Praise for *Bloom (*

"Catriona's positive energy and playfulness wer
Life® trainings she attended with me. In this b   ......es her personal
journey and all the wisdom she has gained over the years with warmth,
humour, and authenticity. She offers you the insights and tools to accept your
own greatness and step boldly into the world. Are you ready?"
—**Patricia J. Crane**, Ph.D., Heal Your Life® Master Trainer

"*Bloom Girl* is a powerful testament to one women's spiritual awakening.
Catriona clearly has a natural gift and ability to clarify the accumulative causes
of suffering in women, releasing stagnant destructive thinking patterns and
equips the reader with the wisdom and life changing tools we need to look at
ourselves and others. Catriona's honesty of her own transformational journey
to self love and acceptance is both deeply moving and inspiring. I truly believe
she has created a unique empowering language of her own that not only Irish
women will relate to and embrace but also women all over the world."
—**Bronagh Gallagher**, singer and actress

"Catriona Jones' book, *Bloom Girl*, outlines a philosophy and toolkit for
women and girls on a journey of self empowerment. The author draws on her
own life experiences, educational training, and work as a life coach, to identify
the internal and external obstacles to human flourishing. She recognises that
patriarchal conditioning impacts all of life and is detrimental to loving oneself
and other people. She makes available her strategies for overcoming the
psychological and emotional impediments to inner and outer freedom, with
additional website links to further useful resources. This book is an important
contribution to our understanding of patriarchal socialisation and provides a
step by step guide for those on the journey to liberation."
—**Dr. Cathy Higgins**, researcher and lecturer

"*Bloom Girl* is an empowering personal story and a rich resource. Catriona
Jones inspires and coaches the reader to honour their dreams and to reclaim
their power to realise them. Catriona's professionalism and compassion shines
through her book."
—**Tonia Browne**, author of the Amazon best-selling
Diving into Life Series and creator of the *Mermaid Diving
into Life Card Decks*, www.toniabrowne.com

BLOOM
Girl

Reclaim Your Goddess Power and Purpose
from Within to Flourish in Life

To my beautiful friend Cheryl,
May the stars continue to
keep us connected & aligned.

CATRIONA JONES

Lots of love from

Catriona xx

x

BALBOA.PRESS
A DIVISION OF HAY HOUSE

Balboa Press books may be ordered through booksellers or by contacting:

Balboa Press
A Division of Hay House
1663 Liberty Drive
Bloomington, IN 47403
www.balboapress.com
844-682-1282

Because of the dynamic nature of the Internet, any web addresses or links contained in this book may have changed since publication and may no longer be valid. The views expressed in this work are solely those of the author and do not necessarily reflect the views of the publisher, and the publisher hereby disclaims any responsibility for them.

The author of this book does not dispense medical advice or prescribe the use of any technique as a form of treatment for physical, emotional, or medical problems without the advice of a physician, either directly or indirectly. The intent of the author is only to offer information of a general nature to help you in your quest for emotional and spiritual well-being. In the event you use any of the information in this book for yourself, which is your constitutional right, the author and the publisher assume no responsibility for your actions.

Any people depicted in stock imagery provided by Getty Images are models, and such images are being used for illustrative purposes only. Certain stock imagery © Getty Images.

Print information available on the last page.

ISBN: 978-1-9822-6887-9 (sc)
ISBN: 978-1-9822-6889-3 (hc)
ISBN: 978-1-9822-6888-6 (e)

Library of Congress Control Number: 2021909821

Balboa Press rev. date: 05/18/2021

Dedication

For Nina
My magical inner child
I love you.

CONTENTS

Bloom
(noun)
A beautiful process of becoming

CHAPTER 1

Purpose

To work with love is to weave the cloth with
thread drawn from your heart.
—Kahlil Gibran, *The Prophet*

Are you ready to believe in yourself and fully bloom in the world?

In the deepest recesses of my heart, this is what I know for sure. Just as flowers bloom into their final forms, we as people have the ability to grow and bloom into our fuller, better, and truer selves. We inhabit a world of divine order. In a universe governed by laws, the exact same laws that organise the beauty and abundance of nature conduct our world too. Laws, when followed precisely, result in pure manifestation of the divine. This is evident in the perfect pitch of birdsong, the warm comfort of a sunset, the beauty and rustle of autumn leaves, and the magic of the floating clouds. We humans are part of this divine plan and consciousness, but we have managed to slip away from our source. We disconnect, leaving a kink in the pipe of flow, and tend to see ourselves as separate. All flowers and nature may have a season to bloom, but not all humans experience the fuller expression of who they truly are. Even though a rosebud in effect is a flower, we don't always witness the fullest manifestation of this miracle in every soul that incarnates on to the planet. We need nature as our teacher to remind us of our sacredness, beauty, innocence, and perfection.

In this book I allow the divine to activate fully within me and express itself through me, bringing me into alignment with my life purpose. I believe I came into this world to inspire and teach. Therefore, I will share with you the tools and techniques to empower you to believe and align and then bloom, to flourish and serve—and to live your best life. These are the same tools that helped transform my life and the lives of many of my clients. I will give them to you in the most straightforward manner, simplest form, and affirm that you will nod willingly and have an aha breakthrough to come into season and fully bloom.

I outline how to shift your self-belief, create a more positive self-image, step into your power, and claim your path in the world. Recalibrating and activating the divine order that is within you, preparing you to embrace the feminine energy of allowing and receiving so the universe can reflect a more beautiful life, a life you deserve. I offer a life filled with harmonious relationships, oozing with creativity, great health, and abundance. It is from this space we create a life filled with inner contentment, an open heart freed from the busy chatter of the mind, and a balanced life in mind, body, and spirit. It brings us back into alignment with the truth of our existence here on earth. The purpose of life is to experience freedom, growth, and joy. You are a *goddess*.

I have worked with women all over the world who have felt at some point in their lives they had betrayed themselves by abandoning their dream lives and dishonoured their true authentic selves, believing they had to settle in an area or several areas of their lives. I, too, was one of those women, simply going through the motions day by day until the discomfort became unbearable. Let us stop the culture of desperation being the driver for women to turn their lives around. Let us create a sisterhood where women learn to honour their desires for all their lives. It is time to start dreaming again and reconnect with that wee girl within who has big plans! Whether you want to take that college course, learn to drive, buy your own house, marry your soulmate, start a new business, or create something amazing in the world, you have all the confidence and everything that it takes. It is simply time to look within and remember. Let go of history and past hurts and disappointment. Do not let past results determine your future. We have all experienced let-downs, disappointments, emotional pain, and been overlooked in promotions. We have been bullied in work, belittled by loved ones, and exhausted ourselves by people pleasing. It is over; this is your time. I see you, I hear you, and I love you. Allow me to hold space for your beautiful heart and your precious dreams.

Let's go, my lovely. It is your time to believe and bloom. I hold to this truth for you until you are willing to step into your full power and claim your space in the world. The feminine energy is the greatest untapped source in the world. It is time to let it flow. Although the future may be feminine, it will only be fantastic when we fully unite as women, as we uncover and reveal your goddess within, giving her full permission to unfold and bloom.

What Do We Mean by Life Purpose?

I want you to hold to this universal truth: You are primarily a spiritual being who has taken a physical form to fulfil a life purpose. When clients come to me and we discuss purpose, they often frequently respond with, 'That's the problem. I don't know what I want to do.' Well, the good news is most people experience confusion or lack of clarity at some stage or stages of their lives, and we all have 'something'! It is just hidden a little deeper inside, and we have to excavate it gently. Let me help you be and connect. We all have the golden thread of purpose woven through our DNA, a purpose that we came in to this world to do. It is something we can do uniquely, in a way that no other can match. When we are aligned with our purposes, we have the potential to light up from the inside and light up everyone else who is in our presence. It's effortless and natural. We all know this state and witness it daily in children. Often enough, the case is that children are usually closer to God and have suffered less confusion and contamination from the outside world. They are still enthused by life, curious, and open.

Deepak Chopra, in his work *The Seven Spiritual Laws of Success,* refers to life purpose as our 'dharma'. He claims that connection to life purpose is a necessary component to success. Purpose in life says we have come into this world, not only with a unique gift, but with the purpose of sharing this talent with others. For every unique talent there is a need for that talent. Otherwise, we never would have been created in the first place. This is the process of supply and demand. We are here to supply. But we have forgotten to trust the demand and need for our gifts and unique talents in the world.

How do you know and how do you discover your true self? I have some great exercises to support you with this or affirm for you what you already know. Only when we come into alignment with this purpose can we access the unlimited abundance, natural rhythm, and ebb and flow that we witness in nature. We then experience the ease and effortlessness of pure potentiality, prosperity, lasting inner peace, joy, and fulfilment. Thus, we join the harmonious dance of life with grace and dignity.

Caroline Myss refers to this as a 'Sacred Contract with God'. She states that we agree and make a pact with God before our souls incarnate into this world on our souls' purposes. I find her work offers a deeply personal experience to journey into the centre of the soul and encounter the ultimate connection with your God. I believe that until we encounter a spiritual awakening with God and our own divinities, it feels as if we are not on the right paths. We often have obstacles to face and emotional pain to process before we connect deeper. This is often referred to by others as 'life lessons', and it is believed in the spirituality of self-development that we continue to face the same lessons and challenges until we learn those lessons and come into alignment with our true authentic selves. This can make perfect sense to anyone who may be experiencing disharmony in an area of her life but cannot quite put a finger on it. You might be in a job with reasonable hours, great pay, and a fair boss but do not experience satisfaction or fulfilment at the end of the day. You just happen to be going with someone else's flow. You are not wholeheartedly connected with your work. Instead, you are repeating the same negative patterns in both relationships and work.

We become tired of the same old, same old, and it no longer serves us or keeps us safe. We acknowledge and accept the understanding that insanity really is repeatedly doing the same thing but expecting different results. Then we shift our consciousness to get into flow, the effortless downstream flow. I remember when I was in my first teaching post in London, the head teacher commented that there was a 'presence' in my classroom. The word 'presence' means 'a state of being'. This observation makes complete sense to me today because at that stage of my journey, it was exactly where I wanted to be as a young, vibrant, primary-school teacher in my early twenties. I felt aligned. My contentment permeated the classroom. It lasted a little while, like most things did at that stage of my life. There have been plenty of jobs and work situations along the way where I just did not want to be there, and I am sure that energy was very apparent too. Seldom do we actually witness people in flow or in their element as humanity has become very disconnected from source. We all play the settling games at some stage in the journey of life.

It is important at this stage that we clarify any confusion around divine, source, or God. The work I share with the world through my teaching and my coaching is spiritual. But it does not belong to any religious denomination; nor does it judge any religious groups. There is one thing that we need to be in agreement with in order to truly bloom: Believe there is a power greater than you and me in this world. The good news is we get to choose its name, whether that be God, creator, angels, energy, source, light, awareness, higher power, nature, Gaia, consciousness, or simply love. We are part of a much bigger picture and fully connected to this power. A drop in the ocean, or maybe even the ocean as the great poet Rumi suggests.

I remember in the early days of my healing journey, I struggled with letting go and handing my life over to a power greater than me. I had become very controlling and was trying to hold on tightly to everything. I believed that holding on to past hurts made me strong. My counsellor, Carole, said to me, 'You cannot control it all. Whether you like it or decide upon it, the sun will rise in the morning.' She was right. Many things were out of my control, and there was a higher power. The penny dropped; the ego was silenced for a moment and I accepted the domain of our spirits, a higher power, and my awareness expanded. Although I could not describe it or make it totally tangible, it felt mysterious, but something holy shifted within me. I relaxed a little, allowed the reins to loosen in my grasp, and became curious about learning to trust the flow of life. I woke up to the understanding that I was more than this body and more than my mind. There was indeed a greater force in the world. Maybe it was safe to relax and get more curious about the spiritual element of life. We all have an awakening experience, a time in life when we woke up to something and became more aware. It is almost like seeing the beauty and the abundance of the world as if for the first time.

Transformation begins with awareness. Several decades ago, Geraint, my husband (boyfriend at the time) and I were backpacking in the Far East. This ought to have been a totally blissful adventure and experience, but I suffered anxiety regularly and struggled with overthinking things. I simply could not relax and enjoy life fully. I was attached to my little bag of worries and continuously fought hard for my limitations. And I had a lot of noise in my head. We were visiting the most spectacular temple complex, the Angor Wats in Cambodia, home to probably the world's most amazing sunsets. The beauty of the carvings was incredible, but I was restless and agitated. One morning I was observing a group of Buddhist nuns in meditation at a temple. They exhibited such peace and grace, and I observed a snippet of their inner peace. In that moment I realised how I yearned for that connection to my soul, to the divine and I was struggling. I felt sad, but the sadness was overshadowed by the immense sense of hope because I thought, *if they can do that, so can I.* There was one thing I knew how to do well and that was to learn.

I set the intention that day in that moment of mixed emotions that I would become a meditator. In that moment of new-found awareness, I set the intention that I, too, would learn to experience stillness and bliss. I can close my eyes today and see and feel the gentle breath of the nuns and their oneness with consciousness. This was a moment of unexpected divine intervention for me, a turning point. All we have to do is remain open and neutral in life. We all have the ability to raise one another up and remind each other the truth of our essence: We are pure love and peace. The happiness and joy of the soul is always ever present, within us.

What Do You Believe?

I encourage you to bring to your awareness a power greater than you that will support your alignment with purpose. You don't even have to name it. Accept or be willing to accept there is a higher power or a co-creator. It might just be a decision to choose love over fear. If you are overthinking, start with the sun. That thought saved my life (more about that later).

Growing up in a Catholic community and spending most of my life in Catholic education, I loved the story of Christmas. In my heart I truly believe that it is a story of an enlightened soul incarnated into this world. This man, Jesus, a great teacher and healer, created a stir and a phenomenon. Whatever other claims religion makes; I believe he was a great person. I do not believe that any religion has the monopoly on Christ, but we all share that divine light within us too. My reason for the inclusion of this story is to share my favourite Bible scene about the magi. During the performance of my fair share of primary-school nativities that I experienced as a pupil, a classroom primary-school teacher, and then as a mother, I have always adored the spectacular scene of the three wise men. As a little girl, I was usually a narrator who stood on the stage. The three kings got to make a grand entrance from the rear of the hall and arrive with opulence and regality. I recall vividly the flow of the velvet gowns, and they had an assistant to carry their trails! The twinkle of their crowns and bejewelled boxes in their hands, no lines to narrate, or to 'learn off by heart' at home. Just a dazzling entrance, and all eyes gazing at their awesomeness. Later in life, whilst teaching in the Middle East, I purchased myrrh and incense in tiny clay pots at a delightful market in Oman. I was dazzled by the exuberance and beauty of the market, the fragrance, colour, and textures of the products. I treasured them for years, later neatly potting them under our Christmas tree until they were finally disintegrating and odourless. I relished the intriguing pageant of the wise ones on camels, foreigners from the East, intuitive and knowing. The wisdom within me was captivated by the manifestations of divine intelligence, but there was no road map or tangible road signs to what this magnetism was all about. Yet.

It was the climax of the show for me (sorry, baby Jesus) although we all knew, 'a King is born.' I would later adore a Christmas card that depicted this scene of the magi bearing gifts or paintings and illustrations of stars, one of which sits on my desk in front of me, *Starry Night Over the Rhone,* by Vincent van Gogh. I love the magic of the stars. They sit in pure alignment, no squabbles or struggles, no discomfort or self-doubt. Just bright lights showing up and shining with ease in the universe. All stars serving equally in the world, playing their parts, unafraid to shine, and lighting up the whole sky for you and me.

As I write now something moves and stirs majestically within me about this divine order. And more so the kings, three wise men, what about them? They were all *knowing,* connected to the divine order of the universe and one consciousness. They followed the star and knew that an enlightened one was incarnating because of their deep connectedness and alignment and trust in the prophecies and one consciousness. I want you to *know* that your beautiful soul, too, has a special divine purpose, a reason for being here, and the world is a brighter place just because you are here. I am not saying we all have the same purpose as Christ, but we all have a purpose, a unique gift and talent to share with the world. A light that can light up the whole sky. In doing so, just as the stars open my heart and connect me with the divine in me, we all have that ability and potential. Why would we cover our lights and play small? There is something that all humans desire, and that is a meaningful life, to grow, and contribute to the world. Because as St Catherine of Sienna said, 'Be who you were created to be, and you will set the world on fire.'

Life can be oh so effortless if we are prepared to get out of our own ways and we get into our own natural rhythms.

Getting to Know Your Purpose

I love to learn and share what I know. This was a behaviour deeply embedded in my life from as far back as I can remember, the age of 5. I would be so enthused with school I would teach what I learnt to anyone who might be willing to listen and learn. One of my most vivid memories is playing school in the kitchen on a Saturday morning. I was so inspired by my week in school, I was often first to rise at home, giving me the freedom to place my chalkboard on the mantelpiece of the kitchen and line my dolls up for Saturday school, so to speak. I can clearly see all these years later how the chalk dust lined the mantelpiece, how I was already connected to my calling. I would teach my dolls until my heart was content. Well, really until the rest of the family would get up. In those days it was a one-room show. The whole family congregated and operated from the kitchen. The whole house back then depended on heat from that one coal fire. Our family huddled around it. It heated the bathwater and dried our clothes. When the kitchen became overcrowded and I was in the way, the school simply relocated to the stairs, the bedroom, or the backyard.

Looking back now, there was something soothing about the kitchen at home. My mother, the strong matriarch of the family, a descendant of strong and powerful matriarchs before her, usually stood at the kitchen sink or bent over the cooker right next to it or wrestling with a twin-tub washing machine at the back door. Those days were a mixture of simplicity and hardship with not even a house telephone, never mind a mobile phone or social media distractions. They were long days, but days that entailed more being than doing. Mindfulness wasn't talked about then but a reality to sit and watch the fire flames flicker, awake to the slightest sound of footsteps, the howl of the wind, or a dog barking in the distance.

Getting up early to play school had the advantages of a little peace and freedom. But one was also often caught to 'read out the fire', not my favourite job in the world. Dust and ashes would escape everywhere from remains of burnt-out fire. Although I enjoyed the process and fine art of lighting the fire, the order of wrapping newspaper methodically, lining the firelighters on top and then the sticks, and magically creating the dancing flames. Unknowingly, the kindling and igniting the fire were simultaneously igniting the fire within me.

There was something reassuring and comforting about an Irish kitchen and your mammy being home in the same place every day after school and the grounding experience of a pot of spuds. But beneath the surface of it all, we were a community steeped in patriarchy and poverty. Nigella Lawson was not licking her lips in our kitchen, but the pounding of the spuds could be heard at the far end of the street. At that time in Creggan, where I grew up (born in the early 1970s), it was regarded as one of the most notorious council estates in Europe. A circle of Irish friends used to joke in later years as we enjoyed the excitement and opportunities of the streets of London, 'If you want to be anything, be an Irish Catholic.' We casually alluded to the guilt and struggle one often experienced in that environment. This was a casual statement I would later have to unravel and explore the depths of and heal to free myself and our children from ancestral limitations.

I want to impress upon you that your past and beginning in life do not determine your future. In fact, they were perfectly staged, like the backdrop of a play, so that you could step into your role and follow your path. Every piece of your story has contributed to your life and serves for a reason on your path and your purpose. I know that some of those pieces may appear oddly shaped and a bit ugly. In fact, too ugly to belong. Trust me; together they are weaving the tapestry of your beautiful life. We do not need more untold stories, unsung heroines, dimmed lights, wounded or abandoned children, or self-betrayed women. Together, united as one consciousness, we yearn for the greatest version of you. It is our time, women of the world, to sparkle and shine brighter than ever. Be seen, and claim your space in the world. The future of the world is the feminine power united.

The opening scene to the heroine's life in my own play looked a bit grey and bleak. Today I love to compare it to the opening of *The Wizard of Oz*, black and white to begin with and then an explosion of magic and colour. Are you ready to embrace the colour palette and gently paint the brushstrokes of your vibrant and more beautiful life, with extra helpings of glitter?

In 1974 in Derry–Londonderry the year I was born into the world, Derry was a town steeped in conflict and daily traumas. The community on both sides, whether Catholic or Protestants—the one of only two boxes you ticked at this time—experienced its own level of hardship. So many people were affected by the conflict at this time, known as 'The Troubles', and thousands of people lost their lives.

As a consequence, during this unrest, dysfunction, and trauma, the price usually came for families in the form of scarcity, poverty, unemployment, lack of industry, discrimination, addiction, paramilitary involvement, imprisonment, violence, and domestic abuse. Conditions inherited and passed on until healed within the family ancestral pattern by the peace and light warriors consciously deciding, 'It ends here with me.' Thankfully, Derry and Northern Ireland has moved through a peace process and the town was awarded City of Culture in 2013. The peace process is with great credit to John Hume, the great architect for peace in Northern Ireland, a selfless soul who constantly worked for the good of community and humanity. Continuous cross-community and reconciliation work takes place in the town today, uniting members of the Derry–Londonderry community. Now a vibrant city that has welcomed his holiness the Dalai Lama several times, we have certainly brought our eyes to the wound and continue to acknowledge it and heal. We recognise the ongoing process of ancestral healing and the reality of the years of suffering.

We are very proud of the talent and success of Derry people and are particularly proud of a unique connection with the Dalai Lama through his friendship with Richard Moore. Richard Moore was 10 years old, walking home from school, when hit and blinded by a rubber bullet fired by an army soldier during the troubles in 1972. Richard never allowed it to hinder his inspirational life, forgiving the soldier that fired the bullet that blinded him. The Dalai Lama called Richard his hero! Derry is indeed full of sung and unsung heroes, and we are super-proud of many of the sons and daughters of Derry. We ooze so much culture and talent and even fame. The voice of Dana with 'All Kinds of Everything'; Rona Downey, actress in *Touched by an Angel*; Bronagh Gallagher, singer and star of *The Commitments;* Phil Coulter with 'The Town I Loved So Well'; and, of course, our fabulous *Derry Girls* by Lisa McGee. There is no end to our stardom. And we are now rising more than ever. This small town is becoming positively huge with the angel wings of our very own Sr Clare Crockett hovering above us and her inspirational teaching to surrender your life to your purpose as given to you by God 'All or nothing'.

The 5-year-old wee girl is instructing her teddies on how to draw the number 5, demonstrating with confidence and unshakable certainty. 'This is the policeman's hat, his neck, and his big belly.' Word for word I mimicked my teacher with a good steady hand and excellent number formation. I was a bright child, one of the eldest in the class. That gave me a great advantage. I was both aware and sensitive. Warm-hearted and helpful. An enthusiastic learner but a somewhat fragile learner too, I was able to pinpoint during my teaching career and study for my master's in education in Wales and my seeking of and dependence on the gold star.

'Stop that talk', my mother exclaimed as she entered the kitchen. I looked confused. 'Don't use that word.' She was referring to the use of 'policeman'.

You see, growing up in Derry, no matter how magical school was, we had the dark cloud of the troubles looming over us daily. My mother, then around age twenty-five, would have been subjected to the hostility, interrogation, and bullying of the forces. She was treated 'less than' in the community and had little faith in authorities and the iron fist of Margaret Thatcher, who just continued to bestow hardships upon young families and the people of Northern Ireland. I had no idea about politics at that time but have clear memories of significant incidents, such as the hunger strikers, the banging of the bin lids, and school milk being abolished. We were aware of injustice and inequalities, experiencing it first-hand, and it came as no surprise that race equality was quick to become a passion of mine. It is a blessing to know and appreciate today that spirit within each of us. Our essential beings have no religion, race, gender, sexuality or ethnicity.

Getting to Know Myself and What I Really Love

School would continue to be a positive experience in my life, and learning continues to inspire and enthuse me and makes my heart sing. Growing up during difficult times, the local library was a magic lamp. We could go anywhere in our minds with a book. As a little girl, I loved to read, devouring books. I would spot new arrivals to the shelves immediately. I loved to complete my lessons and homework. The school day had order, the schedule, timetables, including a milk break and lunch followed by playground fun with friends. The boundaries and consistency, the expansion of my mind was a security blanket and fed my soul. I would learn my spellings by heart every week and gratefully receive my gold star and track my leadership progress across the chart hanging in the classroom, visible to everyone. I was proud to be seen, and I always strove to maintain first place. My stardom didn't rest there. I loved to perform, and I was a competitive gymnast, netballer, and public speaker. If there was an audience and a medal, I was in. I was popular and had lots of friends; I was always a leader and an adventurer. If it wasn't fun or good craic, though, I didn't really stick around for very long. Or I brought the fun if it was welcomed.

I share these achievements not to boast or bore but to open your heart and mind to the little girl within you and what she loves. I want to inspire you to connect with the spirit of your inner child. Remember

Wayne Dyer always said inspire means 'in spirit'. As I share my story and work, I hope to inspire you to become better acquainted with your inner child and reconnect with your talents and gifts. Who exactly is the inner child? We all have imprints of our journeys, stories, and lasting memories in our bodies and hearts. These younger pieces are often close to our original DNA. They can spark great joy, spontaneity, magic, and creativity from within us and connect us with our natural talents. In this book I guide you in supporting any parts of your inner child wounded or abandoned or your inner teenager or young adult who needs reassured, soothed, or comforted through this process of coming into full bloom. Only when we truly step into our stories to heal these pieces can we make peace with our pasts and open our hearts fully to the present moment and the dreams of the future.

Although I was in flow whilst playing the teacher, my sisters continue to laugh and joke about how I always had to be the teacher and was the bossy one! In hindsight, the education system was a tough call too. I alluded earlier that I was a 'fragile learner'. I was always striving to achieve; school for many children growing up during the troubles became a haven. It was consistent and steady in its daily practise but didactic and conformist in its style. A part of me felt both safe and vulnerable. I had high expectations of myself from a very young age, always the achiever, focussed on success, and with a strong emphasis on getting it right. This progressed in later years to perfectionism. I feel our education system helped contribute to that. We were treated like empty vessels that had to be filled with information—sounds, *Peter and Jane* books, multiplication tables, indoor didactic teaching—and you dare not colour outside the lines. I speak not only metaphorically but literally as well.

As a little girl in early education, we were given a sheet to colour in the five little ducks, *Quack, quack*. I am in love with the set-up there. It was an organised classroom, a stimulating environment, and we all had a chair, a personal space, and a pot of coloured pencils to share. I set off swiftly and confidently to work. You see, the approval-seeking wee girl in me has learnt that when she finishes first and gets her work correct, she is acknowledged, seen, and rewarded with—here it comes again—the star, a gold star. However, I made a mistake, and no one at this stage of my journey had reassured me that it was okay to make mistakes; they happen to all humans. Overjoyed about my five yellow ducks coloured beautifully within the lines, my creativity was in flow, and my mind began to wander to the imagined pond surrounding the ducks. I concentrated deeply on my masterpiece and coloured the area around the ducks in a lovely blue. I loved my work and excitedly leapt out of my seat to show the teacher. It appeared to me that it was wrong; I did it wrong! My world crumbled, tears stung my face, and I was devastated. How dare I colour outside the lines. I made her cross, and I wanted to please. Confusion set in, and I was on higher alert. I needed to sharpen my axe. When asked why I was crying, I lied that I felt cold. Creative thinker and quick on my feet. But on reflection, what I really learnt about myself here was how already by the age of 5, I was conforming, put in my box, uncomfortable to express my emotions, not to express my feelings and dishonour me as young as the age of 5. Therefore, perfectly conforming to a very outdated system, like all the women who went before me.

Thereby, my friends, my fragile learner within was born—the programming to conform, stay within the lines. My creative genius was tucked tightly back in, and the star began to hide. It took me years to join these dots, of course, as my natural creativity was somewhat stifled by the educational system and a society that teaches us to conform. The light will only contain itself in confinement for so long until the 'bloom girl' is screaming down our necks and we cannot ignore this calling anymore.

Although my learning experience with the number 5 was somewhat turbulent, the playing school long continued. I loved teaching, speaking, leading, and helping others. That spark was never going to be dimmed because it came from a deeper, more powerful place than any indoctrination or institution could contaminate or tarnish. I am by no means judging the teacher or the school because we teach what we learn. I can honestly say that I made some of the same didactic mistakes in my early teaching career until I understood and learnt better. I had bought into a system that no longer served me. What doesn't kill us makes us stronger. In the words of one of my greatest teachers, Louise Hay, 'We all do the best we can with the understanding we have at that time.' I have been in education almost my entire life—I guess we all have really—and are all the time learning. No school or college has ever taught me the best life lesson ever, self-love and the practice of meditation.

The Enneagram: A Spiritual Tool of Personality Clarity

Discovering the enneagram was a significant piece in affirming my purpose here on earth. It also gave me full permission to be me. Sometimes we can judge ourselves and at times wonder about the way we are. Even though we know and are often reminded that this is how we always were as a child, the self-criticism creeps in when we get caught up on the reaction or response of others towards us. Today I take strength in my behaviour as a child—always the entertainer, performer, leader, and competitor. However, these qualities and traits can often feel like the shadow side to me. For years I found myself judging or criticising myself for my forwardness and relentless desire to achieve and then set the next goal. The enneagram reassured me and gave me permission to take comfort in my gifts and to accept my personality type genuinely. It is a wonderful tool to connect us with our true spirits and essences, letting go of the ego, or what others think we ought to be, and grow personally, socially, emotionally, and spiritually.

Richard Rohr is my go-to leading expert on the enneagram. A renowned theologian teaching spirituality for forty years. I met Father Richard Rohr many years ago, in the late nineties, in England. I was working as a primary-school teacher in London at the time and supporting the work of catechism in our parish. This was my first teaching post in the lovely Dollis Hill, Brent. Brent was a vibrant multicultural melting pot full of many ethnic groups, including Irish, and everyone was welcome. I felt so at home there and valued by the community. Richard Rohr was the keynote speaker for the weekend retreat I attended, and he blew me away. I was mesmerised as he appeared to speak in a whole new language about the cosmos, the universe, and Spirit. I bought the tapes of the weekend and would later play them over and over, captivated by the words of wisdom that flowed from his mouth. His heart was open, soothing, and authentic.

The enneagram is an ancient tool for the discernment of Spirit and personality type. It helped me join the dots and get crystal clear on my purpose and what motivated me. There are nine personality types, and the individual must claim it for herself. It has served me in so many ways, particularly in my love and acceptance of myself, getting to really know and understand me, and to build positive relationships with others. I am grateful to my lovely friend Annmarie for guiding me through this process and holding space as I claimed my personality type 3. As Annmarie eloquently read the list of qualities and described how the number 3 soars like the eagle, is highly optimistic, and self-assured and radiant, tears strolled down my face. I was okay. It was my nature to be ambitious, driven, goal-orientated, approval-seeking, and need to succeed. I came into this world to lead, mentor, and organise. My colour was purple, my flower the rose, and country the United States. My song was 'The Winner Takes It All'. And Oprah Winfrey was a 3! I loved this as I adored her. I hurried home from school as a teenager to watch her show.

I lapped it all up, and it made complete sense. I felt aligned with my goddess within. And it was no surprise to learn that my personality type was heart-centred. There was no oddly shaped piece in this puzzle; it was spot on. I believe the enneagram empowered me to make a quantum leap in my understanding, appreciation, and acceptance of me and my purpose. I was able to make peace with parts of me that often frustrated me or appeared as obstacles to my growth. The question I constantly ask and observe of myself, 'How am I doing?' might always follow me around, and quite frankly, I am good with that. Deep within me, though, I know that self-worth is not created by the opinions of others. It's discovered, remembered, and felt from within.

I include this piece so that you, too, might avail of this wonderful tool. We are all so different, and no type is right or wrong. Regardless of personality, we are all motivated and driven by different things. I think this is also a great tool for leadership and parenting to bring out the best in ourselves and others. Guidance is recommended with this beautiful spiritual process as there are wings to each type, subtypes and characteristics within us whether in or out of alignment. For example, I am a type 3 personality, therefore I dip into the wings and behaviours of both 2 and 4. We have access to all meditation points of the enneagram and are by no means boxed in.

The Enneagram

The Nine Personality Types: Needs, Descriptions, and Job Suitability

1. The need to be perfect: The Reformer and Idealist
   Common jobs: judge, lawyer, police officer, detective, occupational health worker, social worker, environmental specialist, secondary-school teacher, mathematician, statistician, safety specialist, and technician

2. The need to be needed: The Helper and Caregiver
   Common jobs: non-profit leader, therapist, counsellor, humanitarian, religious leader, nurse, special educational needs teacher, human resource manager

3. The need to succeed: The Achiever and Performer
   Common jobs: teacher, mentor, leader, coach, salesperson, physician, executive, actor, athlete, agent, performer

4. The need to be special: The Individualist and Creative
   Common jobs: actor, writer, artist, personal trainer, dance instructor, hairdresser, photographer, designer

5. The need to perceive: The Investigator and Thinker

Common jobs: engineer, computer programmer, scientist, mathematician, author, scholar, technician, analyst

6. The need for security: The Loyalist and Hard Worker
    Common jobs: occupational health and safety specialist, security guard, environmental scientist, construction and building inspector, fire inspector

7. The need to avoid pain: The Enthusiast and Adventurer
    Common jobs: artist, travel writer, interior designer, photographer, bartender, tour guide, travel agent

8. The need to be against: The Challenger and Protector
    Common jobs: lawyer, politician, director, financial manager, business owner, marketing strategist, sales director

9. The need to create harmony: The Peacemaker and Mediator
    Common jobs: counsellor, social worker, veterinarian, diplomat, editor, therapist, healthcare professional, librarian

In acknowledging your type, it can support your understanding of suitable job types and purpose and avoid struggles and difficulties. If you are unsure of your purpose, it will certainly guide, affirm, or confirm your work in the world. You can learn more at www.ennegraminstitute.com. Robert Holden offers inspirational teaching on the basic anatomy of the nine personality types and the timeless wisdom of the enneagram to help you experience practical growth and transformation. You can learn more at www.robertholden.com.

What Did Your Tribe Say?

I love to teach. It makes me feel alive, and I feel so fulfilled when clients and students wake up and grasp something. Eyes light up just like stars popping out to say hello from the night sky. Something would click, a realisation happens, or there would be an aha moment. My personal journey of self-development and my work as a coach have taught me the art of blending your purpose with creativity. We are conditioned to old programming. When we come from a place of lack and scarcity, we learn to make do and be grateful for what we have. If a job was available you took it, no picking and choosing. A nine-to-five job and an opportunity to slog your guts out at the grind were luxury and a pleasure only bestowed to a few in a working-class and a socially deprived community.

These harsh lessons on lack and scarcity must be undone, so to speak, letting go of the hustle mentality. It can be a tough shift to make from this mentality to one of abundance. It involves learning to trust the process and borrowing the belief of someone who has already dug the trenches, laid the tracks, and blazed the trail. When I qualified as a primary-school teacher, I broke many patterns within my family system. I continue to create new positive paradigms today. It was the tradition for women to leave school, set immediately to work in the shirt factory, and marry; many would start a family as young as 17 years old. I recall watching the ladies happily chatting on their way to work, dressed in their overalls, and walking to work with pride. The Derry shirt factory women provided renowned work in terms of quality. But I never felt this was the path for me. This was a thriving industry and brought great money into the family home, a blessing for a mother with several daughters. I wanted to teach, go to university, and study. In following our paths, it sometimes feels we are breaking the traditions of our families and communities.

All families and cultures have their own belief systems around jobs, work, women, and family. That system can really grip the first chakra located at the base of your spine, the invisible energy field that we cannot see, but for some it is felt. It comes from hard and fastidious rules. It's the rules of, 'We don't do it like that in this family.' The ancestral story passed down. In conforming we lose our own personal identities and essences, and we slip away from our original purposes. Understanding the energy field has really helped me clear negative energy and reclaim my power from within. This is where your baseline programming is stored and held. Undetected and cleared from blockages can manifest as dis-ease in the body, usually with the first chakra. For women, this often appears as IBS, colitis, or other digestive issues.

I admire and follow the work and teachings of Dr Christiane Northrup, and it was a snippet of heaven to be present when she escorted Louise Hay onstage at Louise's ninetieth birthday celebration in San Diego. I was proudly seated with other global Heal Your Life Teachers and acknowledged on that day for our work in the world. These two women are indeed two powerhouses in the industry of self-development and inspirational women who forged the path for all of us. Christiane Northrup, a gynaecologist and spiritual guru, spearheads work about everything that can go right in the wisdom of a women's body. She challenges patriarchy head-on and highlights the ancestral benefits of the woman's healing journey. I agree with her claim that every woman who heals herself helps to heal all the women who came before her and all those who follow her. Break the cycle of playing small, of women losing their identities in the midst of family life and careers. Women for generations have felt they have to compromise in life and cannot have the family life and the successful career. We are ready to rise and embrace the art of delegating with grace.

I believe that the reason most women never step into their full power and align with their true purposes is the fear of breaking tribal patterns and expectations of what others will think. I implore you to dig deep into your power, and take this path in honour of you and the entire woman in your life, family, community, and globally. There is a feminine revolution, and we can be at the forefront. Stop worrying what other people want and how they expect you to behave. That paradigm is now obsolete. It is time to bloom, girl. My personal healing journey and self-development have empowered me to teach and work in a way on my terms, honouring my desires. I still fulfil my purpose to teach but in a flexible, creative blend of what I love to do and how I love to do it, creating balance and joy in my everyday life. Today I look at my schedule and love and approve of every entry jotted in with my well-loved pencil. Make your schedule your new BFF.

A period of suffering or emotional pain is often experienced before we actually decide and commit to honouring ourselves in the world. Most people will experience this at some stage of their lives. Believe me, I have had my fair share of pain, too, so you are not alone. Whether you have lost a job, been bullied in work, exiled in a community, or betrayed by a loved one, you can turn the story around and make the comeback even better than the setback. All the obstacles that were seemingly put in your path were simply God redirecting you to a bigger and better life. You were too big and bold for that situation, person, work, or place. Trust the movement and shift, change of direction. And there is one thing I am more certain of today: Strong, powerful women with moral compasses are not always welcome within every tribe. Rise anyway. Take a stand for positive transformation for the good of all.

When we totally align with our hearts' desires, we stop worrying about what we think other people are thinking about us. We let go of asking, 'What's in it for me?' and have an authentic and deep desire to serve others. We join in the beautiful cosmic dance and effortless flow of the universe. In opening our hearts to the unlimited abundance available in the world, undo the old programming, clear the root chakra of tribal beliefs that no longer serve us, we welcome a long-awaited paradigm shift and enjoy prosperity in all areas of our lives. You see, when you incarnated into this world, another star was born. Follow your star like the magi, and do not look back or worry what other people are thinking. Chances are they're not thinking at all—at least not about you!

My Client: From Exhausted Hairdresser to Vibrant Holistic Therapist and Coach

When Helen first came to work with me, she was overweight, hunched over in posture, and suffering from anxiety and chronic back pain. 'I don't know what's wrong with me,' she said. 'I have a great business, and the salon never stops. I love my clients, and I don't mind hairdressing. We have no children and no great pressure or stress.' Helen was burnt out physically and emotionally because she had a wee voice in her head and a deep yearning niggling her every day. It was taking its toll on her health and well-being. She felt that she was over eating and drinking too much wine in the evening. 'My husband doesn't know what to do with me, and I am sick and tired of moaning.'

I guided Helen to reconnect with her body and learn to press pause and fall still. My Zen tools allowed her to examine and reflect on what she loved, and she opened up about her dreaded Sunday-evening-blues-conflicted passion for spirituality and holistic therapy. Within months, Helen closed the salon, trained in holistic therapy treatments, and opened a brand-new practice. She shed the extra pounds, created the business of her dreams, and continued to connect with others on a deep, meaningful level in a safe and sacred space. She could now choose her schedule and get paid her worth, what she deserved.

As women, we have an incredible feminine creative energy. If this energy is restricted, stifled, or monotonous, our energy will be out of balance and take its toll on the body and mental health. We tend to give and forget to receive. I share with you in this book the exact tools I use with my clients so that they can consciously design and create their dream jobs. You can too.

I use a holistic approach in the work I do with my clients whilst connecting to the body. I suggest becoming aware of your energy field and chakras for simple everyday living. Although the human energy system is said to have many chakras, I refer to seven in my work and when I teach meditation. The Eastern traditions name these seven chakras as the main energy centres of the body. They are placed at different points of the spinal column and are considered responsible for the flow of life energy. I have collated some information if it is of interest to you, and will talk more about unblocking chakras and how this can impact and enhance your personal development.

Many of my clients enjoy the use of healing crystals and essential oils to help balance, relax, and sooth. All crystals and oils vary in terms of use and applications. Guidance is recommended, particularly during pregnancy.

Chakra Well-Being

Chakra	Location	Colour and Element	Association	Physical Connection	Crystal	Healing Process and Affirmation
1 Root	Base of spine	Red Earth Grounded	Tribal beliefs, power, sex, and money (fight, flight or freeze)	Adrenal glands	Red jasper Bija mantra Lam	Releasing frustration, tribal guilt. Allows manifestations. I am grounded and centred, and it is safe for me to honour my purpose.
2 Sacral	Lower belly	Orange Water In flow	Personal relationship with sexuality, sensuality, and creativity	Ovaries and testes	Carnelian Bija mantra Vam	Releases anger. Allows creative flow and pleasure. I feel safe and connected to my power within.
3 Solar plexus	Belly (above the belly button)	Yellow Fire Self-mastery	Self-esteem and self-worth (the sun)	Stomach, kidneys, liver	Yellow calcite Bija mantra Ram	Releases fear and anxiety. Enhances energy, confidence, and courage. I do good in the world with confidence and courage.

Chakra	Location	Color / Element / Quality	Focus	Gland / System	Crystal / Bija mantra	Affirmation
4 Heart	Above the heart (bridge between earth and Spirit)	Green / Air / Love	Love and compassion	Thymus gland / Immune System	Green aventurine / Bija mantra Yam	Releases apathy. Allows love. I love and approve of myself and others.
5 Throat	Throat	Blue / Ether/Space / Purification	Expression and communication	Parathyroid glands	Sodalite / Bija mantra Ham	Releases misunderstanding. Allows clear communication. I speak my truth with love and grace.
6 Third Eye	Between the eyebrows	Indigo / Light / Mind	Intuition and vision (sixth sense)	Pituitary gland	Amethyst / Bija mantra OM	Releases confusion/ignorance. Allows knowledge and true will. I see clearly now from a place of calm and trust.
7 Crown	Top of head	Violet-white / All that is thought/cosmos	Clarity, wisdom, and higher states of consciousness	Pineal gland	Clear Quartz / Bija mantra Silence (we just listen)	Releases obsession. Allows calm and divine guidance. I know and understand that I am divinely guided and have a soul purpose on earth.

Bloom Girl Exercise 1

What Is Your Purpose?

In order to connect with our purpose, we need to connect with the divine and Spirit within you. This is achieved in stillness, by simply being present in the moment.

Press Pause

Sitting in an upright position, back straight, two feet on the ground and relax the shoulders.

Take three deep, clearing breaths.

Keep two feet flat on the ground, body uncrossed.

Ensure your chin is parallel to the floor.

Gently close your eyes, and allow your breath to settle down and find its own natural rhythm.

Connect with your sense of hearing. What sounds do you hear?

Connect with your sense of smell. What fragrances do you smell?

Connect with your sense of taste. What can you taste?

Connect with your sense of touch and the play of air on your skin or touch of clothing, hands resting on the lap.

As you connect to all your senses and experience a sense of relaxation, you can either repeat—quietly and inwardly to yourself—the word, 'peace'.

Or

The affirmation, 'I am calm.'

Or

The mantra, 'So hum'.

Eckhart Tolle says,

> When you lose touch with inner stillness, you lose touch
> with yourself. When you lose touch with yourself, you
> lose yourself in the world.

Explore Joy

1. Bring your attention to your body, and particularly your heart chakra.
2. Write the word 'joy' in the centre of a page, and quietly repeat the word to yourself.
3. Record anything that brings you joy, makes your heart sing, and lights you up.

This exercise will begin to bring you into alignment with your essence and dharma.

Now take a few moments to journal and reflect what you loved to do as a little girl, your inner child. This is a gentle exercise. Go as far back as you can recall. Do you remember your early school days, a favourite game, song, or toy? You must not worry yourself or get frustrated. Allow the memories and pieces to arise gently from the sacred space of stillness.

You can continue to build on this exercise as we journey along together. More ideas will arrive into your consciousness. Trust the flow. Avoid any negative chatter that pops up, and hold to the truth that you have a purpose; you are here to supply a demand. Look always to the heart for this piece. It knows the way.

Bloom Girl Exercise 2

Reflect in your journal.

What did you learn about education and work growing up?

Summary

Remember, bloom girl:

- You are a primary spiritual being who has taken physical form to fulfil a purpose.
- Your inner child will reconnect you with your heart.
- The heart will signpost the way to your joy, joy is the ultimate seed to plant for success in life.

You can download my complimentary Life Purpose Guided Meditation and your own personal Bloom Girl Workbook at www.catrionajones. com/bloomgirl.

CHAPTER 2

Desire

Man's right to life means his right to have the free
and unrestricted use of all the things which may be
necessary to his fullest mental, spiritual and physical
unfoldment: or, in other words, his right to be rich.
—Wallace D. Wattles

What do you love and really want in your life? Does life
sometimes feel unfair to you? Do you still feel you are
not getting what you need or want? Perhaps you flirted
with the law of attraction, read *The Secret,* got super-excited, and then
gave up because nothing seemed to work. Maybe you feel like you
haven't followed through on your promises, not managed to shift the
extra weight, find a new job, work on that new side hustle opportunity,
activated the new gym membership, stick to date night with your
partner, and telling yourself repeatedly, 'I'll start on Monday.' All the
while the running tape in your head is reminding you that you are
a failure. You bully yourself daily with a long list of your unfulfilled
promises.

Life really is supposed to feel good, and one's natural state is happiness.
As little babies we were so open to life and in awe of everything. Our
daughter at just a few months old was fascinated by the discovery of

29

her hands. Do you ever notice how impressed small children are when they see themselves in the mirror? Everything is wonderful. The only time most babies cry is to communicate when they are tired or hungry or need a nappy changed. When a toddler falls over, the child cries for a few moments but is quickly reassured and returned to a happy state. Children don't dwell or wallow in sadness for very long. They pick themselves up and continue to crawl, walk around the furniture, explore, and walk again.

I love to listen to Robert Holden talk about happiness. In fact, he created a whole project about it called The Happiness Project. He illustrates how the language we use to describe when we feel happy is often associated with negative connotations and pain. Comments such as, 'I am dying to meet with you', 'We had a hell of a time', or, 'She is drop dead gorgeous.' Another phrase we use here in Ireland when referring to someone of sound nature is, 'She is dead on.' How interesting that we choose language of death and decay to describe positive experiences. Old programming of negativity, avoidance of the expression of joy or elation, and if you were Irish Catholic, you were probably told, 'You will cry for all that laughing.' You will actually if you believe it to be true. Or you can ride the wave of positivity and accept the better life gets, the better it gets, and there is an upward spiral too.

The process of asking with clarity is about becoming really conscious of our desires and the everyday language and thoughts we share with the universe. In this chapter I guide you through the law of attraction. Every component that makes up your life is indeed drawn to you by the powerful law of vibration and attraction. Thus, it is critical from the outset that we get the asking stage and the focus of our attention and desires crisp and on point. To brisk over this initial stage is like the gardener forgetting to disperse the seeds into the fertile ground. It is a three-step process of ask, believe, receive. It's a simple one, yet we certainly can overcomplicate or even omit stages along the way. It is important to get crystal clear on the asking and refine the details daily. Decide what you really want, and the universe will meet you there. For once, let it be easy.

I will discuss these steps in the next three chapters.

Chapter 2—Ask: What do you desire?

Chapter 3—Believe: Story Patterns - What are your limiting beliefs, and what do you need to start believing as truth?

Chapter 4—Receive: Align to allow.

Step 1: Ask—What Do You Desire?

Everything in our world originated in thought.

> In the beginning was the word, and the Word was with
> God and the Word was God. (John 1:1)

The Bible is outlining the manifesting process here. All of creation began with a thought, then words and actually into physical form. I want to support you in understanding and mastering this process and experience the magic of these universal laws. We are the creators of our lives, and you can change the content of your story starting now. Initially when clients come to see me or I open a dialogue in a workshop with an audience or during an event, there is a lull sometimes between the question of 'What do you want?' and the answer. More times than enough the question goes unanswered. Many people, busy working mums particularly, lack clarity about what they want. In a world that is busy and chaotic—with constant downloads from work, relationships, social media, a demanding education system, getting caught up in the supposedly 'dream life' of celebrities (who appear to have it all together)—the reverence of connecting with oneself and stillness is becoming a rare opportunity or experience in daily life. As women, we often have put ourselves on the bottom of the list of desires and understandably struggle to answer this question. We have become mere servants or martyrs to the hecticness of life and run ragged to meet the needs of everyone but ourselves, almost to the extent that busyness has become our status quo. No one ever asks us what we need or want.

But more important, the key point here is that we have stopped asking it of ourselves. Somewhere along the journey we engaged in a self-abandonment process until we decide busy is boring and no fun.

Self-doubt sneaks up on the best of us as we get caught up in the 'analysis paralysis' of our everyday lives. How good am I performing at work? Am I a good mother, wife, daughter, sister, employee, friend, neighbour? We have so many roles and hats to wear, we can feel we are not serving any of them fully or adequately. Women often internalise the belief that we are nothing but a hot mess, sometimes holding it together with sugar, caffeine, or wine, or perhaps all the above. We get swept up in what we start to believe was our perfect lives and abandon the dreams of the little girl within who always had a spring in her step and a brand-new idea. Let's not go down the road of judgement or self-criticism. Instead, fire up that creativity and spontaneity, fearlessness and curiosity once again. Where did we lose our power, and where did that fire in the belly go?

It is time to untie the shackles of serving and suffering. Stop neglecting yourself; fill your own cup first. I have worked with hundreds of women who suffered from burnout and feeling overwhelmed. 'Self-care' is a word and habit talked about in the self-development industry, but how can we make that tangible in our lives? I encourage you to stay in the heart centre here, and reconnect with the joy you activated in chapter 1. Learning to ask for your desires is a huge step. For many women, it is a breakthrough to communicate how they honestly feel, validating you and your worthiness in the world. There is nothing more beautiful than a woman unafraid of her vulnerability, a woman with a pure heart and good intention open to receiving.

This is the perfect opportunity to reset your inner compass. The needle is pointing towards joy, and we are fully present to beautiful you. Where are you at today, and where do you want to be? We are moving on from just doodling and pondering and liking uplifting quotes on social media to wholeheartedly making decisions and asking *you* what your perfect day would look like.

The contrast of what you don't want might be more prevalent here, and we can use that too. It is helpful to support you to pivot to what you do want. If you were or are a netballer like me, you sure know how to pivot. Pivoting allows you to travel in any direction.

Imagine waking up every morning enthused about your day and looking forward to your work. You never have to worry about time, money, or what other people think of you ever again. You have a self-love program that grounds you, energises you, and connects you with inner contentment and abundance every day. You feel loved and have respect and kindness for everyone. Every day you bloom even more than the day before, opening up and flourishing.

Children are great teachers of how to ask, how to persist, and how to never give up. If you have ever doubted the power of repetition or persuasion, look to a child with a demand. I smile to myself as I begin discussing this topic of asking and desire. I recall picking our son up from school one day when he was about 10 years old. He looked at me, smart and alert, present and attentive, reading me, and checking my form. 'Can I have a chocolate kinder egg?' he asked. I said yes immediately and in a relaxed manner. Straight in with a response, he said, 'Can I have two?' Of course, my answer was no, but I love this memory. It clearly demonstrates the inhibitions—or lack of inhibitions—of children. They are unafraid to pile up their list of desires. And just when you think that's it, the list is complete, they add even more. Particularly at Christmastime, when you think you are ahead of yourself and all ready for Santa coming! How many times have you decided in your head the answer to their demand is *No*, but before you know it, you hear yourself say yes? We give in to their powerful persuasion and their persistence, responding to new tactics, expressions, and dances of insistence until their demands are met.

It is time for us to relearn and remember how to ask. It is time to tap into our very own persistence and consistency. Believe and receive, so we can once again attract more wealth, better health, and happiness into our lives. And ditch the self-defeating, soul-destroying mantra of, 'I'll start on Monday.'

The law of vibration and attraction has not failed us. We have simply stopped asking and receiving; we've abandoned our hearts' desires. As adults, we set limitations for ourselves on what we can and cannot have. When did we stop asking and dishonouring what lights us up? We can be too quick as women to become passive and say, 'What's the point?' and park our needs. Begin with the little things today, and put yourself back in the game of life. Enjoy your favourite beverage, light a candle, eat a cake, or read a chapter in your favourite book.

It is our time to rise and persist. Keep on just keep on, asking like children until the yes appears. Jack Canfield says there is always a yes out there. He is one of the most inspirational and persistent authors I have heard of. His co-authored book *Chicken Soup for the Soul* was rejected by 144 publishers before he got his yes. Can you even imagine that number of nos?

Too often we give up at the first hurdle and create a pattern of not consistently holding steadfast to our dreams. Sometimes it is when the fruits of our efforts are about to appear that we throw in the towel. I have witnessed this time and time again in my own journey and breakthrough and with clients. Just as we claim we can't be bothered— 'What is the point?'—the miracle happens. It is time for you to develop a mindset and certainty like Canfield's. Clarify what you really want and not just ask but demand it, as Peggy Mc Coll instructs us to do so in her recent book, *The Demand Principle*. I love her certainty and authority on manifesting. She says that all you have to do is know what you want and demand it. And demand more of yourself. Peggy explains that you don't have to know how you will bring your desire into your reality when you decide what you want. Simply trust that when a desire reveals itself to you, it comes from the source, the universe.

When you decide, remember to make the decision based upon how you feel and ignore 'logic' or 'good

excuses' as to why you cannot or should proceed.
(Peggy McColl, *The Demand Principle*)

Take a few moments to connect with the decision to ask and the uplifting emotion your desires bring. Embed and consider self-care at this stage to create the optimum environment. Self-care is an act of self- love. In filling our cups first, everyone benefits. And as the saying goes, 'When Mammy is happy, everyone is happy.' To be with your desires is the most beautiful decision you can make at this stage. In my programme Self-Care 101, I pose the question, 'What is the most loving and nurturing thing I can do for myself today?' Here is a list of the top 10 responses gathered from some of the women I have worked with that might help you create the ambience to relax and drop into your heart, connecting with your pleasure and desires and reconnecting with your deservability.

Self-Care 101

1. Have a luxurious bath.
2. Buy yourself flowers.
3. Book a massage.
4. Take a gentle walk in nature.
5. Journal your gratitude and appreciation.
6. Light a candle for you.
7. Spritz your favourite aroma.
8. Play your favourite tune.
9. Laugh out loud.
10. Give yourself a hug.

Self-Care Inner Dialogue to Thyself

1. It is safe for me to say no rather than yes.
2. I turn my shoulds into coulds.
3. I am enough.
4. Everything is working out perfectly.
5. I make great decisions.
6. I am strong.

7. No voice is louder than my inner voice.
8. I treat myself with compassion today.
9. I have so got this; let it be easy.
10. I see you, I hear you, I love you.

These practices and affirmations promote self-love, boost confidence, improve attitude, encourage motivation, and build a positive self-image.

My Story

I was born one of six children. There were five girls and one boy; I was the second eldest. Growing up times were tough, as I mentioned earlier, and we struggled as a family some weeks to make ends meet. There was little employment available in our community, where many of us bought into a massive story of lack and scarcity. My mother made endless lists of what she needed with a frown on her face and notes made on the back of strips made from cardboard boxes. There always seemed to be a new baby on the way, and the cloth would have to be cut again. Luxury and opulence were foreign entities.

How we view family life as a child has a huge impact on desire and deservability. Everyone in the same family can have completely different experiences and perceptions. My mother often talked about how she felt she had two families when we were growing up because there were several years between baby number 3 and baby number 4. On reflection, with my mother's theory in mind, I got to experience life as the middle child during this first family period. I often notice in photographs how my older sister would be sitting close to our mother, and the younger sister on our father's knee. I would float in the middle, the evolvement of little miss independent and self-reliant, always the freedom-seeker. From this early stage, each of us begin to create an invisible pecking order in our heads that might be real and a belief held only by you. However, it creates the belief system and conditioning that determine our attitudes and visibility in the world, as well as the self-images we hold. So, you can imagine that by the time three more children arrived, I emerged as a strong big sister in family number 2. I was Mammy's helper and a mini-mammy by the age of 10. There was always someone ahead of me in need of attention.

Where did you fall in your family's dynamics? What role did you step into and willingly accept as a little girl and for whom?

The belief systems we take on permeate and penetrate our worlds. We hold onto and grasp them so strongly because they are familiar. We even end up fighting for our limitations and making our wounds our identities until we consciously wake up having had enough of the victim mentality.

I vividly remember leading the race on my school's sports day when I was 10 years old. I was coming in strong and about to finish in first place. Consciously I wanted to win, but now I understand how my subconscious mind was deciding the result for me. I slowed down enough to allow the girl behind me to overtake me and finish first, making me second place. I can remember this event as clear as yesterday, and it happened over three decades ago. The paradigm of I am not number one was embedded into my subconscious, and already my programming, rather than my desires and potential, was dictating the results.

This was just how it was then, how it was supposed to be. And my process of taking care of others put me in the role of a carer and helper. My mother was one of fifteen children, and my father one of twelve. Being born into a big Irish family gifted me with great organisational skills, confidence, leadership abilities, resourcefulness, and practicality. However, somehow amidst the busy family life, I lost my voice, my power, my ability to express what I really desired and to be totally visible in the world.

It wasn't always there as an option. You simply had to 'Be grateful for your lot.' Growing up during hard economic times can leave us feeling guilty or even ashamed when we do have needs, requests, or desires. There was a limit to what you could have, and many of your belongings were second-hand. So, did I first struggle with asking? Absolutely. The concept of, 'Let it be easy', was way out of my reach and intangible.

The discomfort of not achieving my full potential, like the memory of not achieving the well-deserved gold medal in athletics, eventually became too painful. We all have memories of not making it, not being chosen, or being overlooked. The human spirit can only accept defeat and only play small for a limited amount of time. We were made for greatness. We are all spiritual beings, and it is natural for us to want to expand. Lack of growth and contributions in the world will frustrate us and eventually become emotionally painful. Spirit will always be for expansion; it's our divine nature. Anais Nin said,

> And the day came when the risk it took to remain tight in the bud was more painful than the risk it took to blossom.

Never be afraid to bloom, my lovely. Borrow someone else's belief, and get to work on your deservability. We have so many inspirational women in the world that turned their stories around, shifted the paradigms that no longer served them, and created the lives they desired. Some of my inspirational role models are Louise Hay, Oprah Winfrey, Peggy McColl, Ruth Bader Ginsburg, Michelle Obama, and J. K. Rowling. Women who prove no matter where you begin your life, whatever disadvantaged circumstances you found yourself in, no matter what curveballs you think have been thrown in your direction, when you have held steadfast to a vision, like a dog with a bone, it has to manifest into form. Adopt the energy of strong, powerful women, and see them standing around you, locking in together as a group, and cheering you on as you claim first place on the podium. Winning in life your style and interpretation of success.

The Universal Laws

At this point I want to outline the seven natural laws of the universe to embed into your study and development. You may already be familiar with them, and now might be a great time to revisit and study deeper the Seven Great Hermetic Principles. As a student I never studied science as it didn't appeal to me. The paradigm told me science was for boys, and quite frankly I thought that I didn't understand any of it. Many students of self-development believe that the law of attraction is a secret when in fact it is pure science.

All of life is governed by these same laws. The law of vibration is what we really want to concern ourselves with initially. This is the primary law that determines the law of attraction. I endeavour to study them and understand them deeper every day. In looking to nature and young children, we are given evidence of these laws close to source in motion. Nature reminds us of the abundance of life, and we originated from the same essence that created nature. Through the experience of meditation, we uncover the true self that lies at the core of each and every one of us. I will simply outline them and refer to them throughout the book to support your journey of growth and manifestations.

The Seven Universal Laws

1. The Law of Perpetual Transmutation
    The law of perpetual transmutation says everything is always moving, and nothing rests. Know things are moving and changing all the time. We all have the ability to change our world through thought and manifest thought into physical form.

2. The Law of Relativity
    Nothing is big; nothing is small. It's only how you relate to it. There may always be someone smarter, prettier, taller, and richer than you in the room.

3. The Law of Vibration
    Everything is energy; it moves and vibrates. Every thought vibrates a signal and attracts a matching signal, one that is on the same frequency. The law of attraction is about choosing thoughts that are consistently in alignment with your desires.

4. The Law of Polarity
   Everything is dual, has poles, and has a pair of opposites. Good and bad, whatever end you choose to focus on you make bigger. Choose happy, positive, uplifting stories.

5. The Law of Rhythm
   Everything has a natural cycle and energetic flow, like a swinging pendulum. The tide comes in and goes out, the sun rises and sets. Accept the ebb and flow of life.

6. The Law of Cause and Effect
   The law of cause and effect states that for every action there is a cause and a reaction, often referred to as karma. All thought is creative and has an effect. Consistently focus on your desires. Thoughts are like seeds that are planted in your mind and bloom into physical form.

7. The Law of Gender (Gestation)
   The law of gestation states that everything takes time to manifest. Everything has a beginning and grows into form as more energy is added to it. Stay focussed, and trust the invisible growth of your goals beneath the soil and divine timing.

My Client

Aly was a corporate lawyer in London. She was overwhelmed and burnt out. She was a high achiever and always delivered outstanding results in work. She wanted the best for her children and was struggling to hold on to a relationship.

When Aly started to work with me, she explained how she started her day exhausted by hitting the snooze button, running on empty, and felt she had no balance in her life. Aly was tired of compromising her own well-being, and her life lacked balance. Family and friends were worried about her.

When Aly and I sat down together and really gave attention to her heartfelt desires, a sense of calm and hope began to arise from the shift of attention to focusing on what she did want. Aly became a serious student of the mindfulness tools I recommended, and the Zen toolkit (the exact Zen toolkit is outlined in chapter 4) helped her adopt a more positive attitude, connect with the present moment, and become self-aware. She was able to regulate her emotions and energy. Aly found it particularly important to follow her heart for peace of mind. She embedded my morning ritual recommendations and really began to own her day.

As we reflected on her transformation, we were in agreement that the freest people in the world are those who have inner peace. Something magically shifts when we decide to hold a sacred space for our own heartfelt desires. The power shifts in the decision-making, in deciding enough is enough.

Flower of Life, the unfolding.

Let's meet you where you are at, not someone else's idea of where you should be.

Consider the areas of your life where you want to create change. You might find the flower of life supportive for this exercise as a baseline to get you started. You can download your own personal copy at www.catrionajones.com/bloomgirl.

The flower encourages you to consider your personal contentment in the following areas:

- Family and friends
- Money
- Health and well-being
- Romantic relationships
- Career and life purposes
- Service and community
- Joy and creativity
- Personal development

Imagine Your Dream Life

I have great certainty that feeling is the secret ingredient to success, that and beginning with the end picture in sight. Let go of any doubt at this stage. Allow your imagination to be carried away in your dream life, remembering vibrational law. This is your time to paint the picture of exactly how you desire things to be. I love Gina De Vee's attitude towards asking. She is audacious and encourages women to think and behave like queens. We all have that royal lineage flowing to and through us. In her book *The Audacity to Be Queen,* Gina writes,

> In every woman lives a Queen. She is smart, feminine, powerful, generous, visible, prosperous, and usually has a great sense of humour. Though she has, enjoys, and requires great material wealth, she doesn't bow to it, nor does she lord it over others. Instead, she lives a life worthy of her calling.

A queen never denies her ability or her worth in the world. And why would you? We are and man is (as in woman too) God's highest and greatest creations. It is time to get out of your own way and dream bigger than ever. Get carried away.

The more emotionally involved you become with your goals, the quicker you will manifest it into form; success loves speed. Remember that your mind doesn't know the difference between imaginative and real. Feel, connect, and impress upon your subconscious everything you truly desire. Use your senses to evoke this impression and experience now. Revisit this outcome of your desires over and over again, but particularly first thing in the morning and the last thing at night. Refine the picture's details as if you were giving someone instructions on how to paint it! Imagine it as though it were already complete.

> When your understanding grasps the power to visualize your heart's desire and hold it with your will, it attracts to you all things requisite to the fulfilment of that picture by the harmonious vibrations of the law of

attraction. You realize that since Order is Heaven's first law, and visualization places things in their natural element, then it must be a heavenly thing to visualize. (Genevieve Behrend, *Your Invisible Power*)

I love this! Full permission to move away from the grindstone and relax. Let go of the addiction to struggle—which we all experience. Just visualise it. But of course, we still need to take inspired action; I will have more on that later. All you have to do right here, right now is to be with your dreams! Get into the vibe. This is where the scientific results are at.

See yourself in perfect health, feel the emotion of the prosperous bank statement, the romantic relationship, the beautiful sunsets, the view from your new home, the vitality of your healthy body, the reverence of peace of mind, inner contentment of doing a job you love. See and feel yourself in your element, in flow and a full expression of the divine intelligence and power within you.

As we plant the seeds, we already visualise them in full bloom. Accept it all as possible. Adopt the, 'If she can do it, so can I,' belief. See it in your mind's eye, imprint it in your heart, and you will create it in your life.

How We Manifested Our New Home

Sometimes we have to take things to the creative and the illogical to manifest. When we first relocated back to Ireland, we were living in rented accommodations. Anyone who is renting or has rented knows when you have that goal for your own home it can sometimes get to the point of desperation. Tony Robbins, world-renowned self-development guru, said we achieve our goals out of, 'inspiration or desperation'. It had been almost four years, and we still had not managed to buy our new home. There were lots of reasons and stories created in my mind for this: Our property in Wales was rented to good tenants, we were still relatively new to all our income streams coming from self-employment, and the estate agents were cliquey. The banks had really tightened the lending process, and we struggled to deliver the necessary proof in paper. Anything other than perhaps we needed to really focus on the outcome and connect with the vibe of seeing it already complete. This involved seeing ourselves packing, moving, unpacking, and connecting with the feelings and joy. Letting go of all stories around obstacles was critical. We shifted our energies to the assumption that it was already happening.

My husband often came home and mentioned houses he saw up for sale in different areas. There was so much variation on our dialogue around houses. We would move from town houses to beach houses, new builds to period homes! It dawned on me that we were sending mixed message to the universe. We needed to lock in together as a family and be crystal clear about what our new home would look like. We were clear we wanted a house in a fairly rural, quiet area near the beach, and not too far from town. It would be detached with a garden but located in a street so the children had friends to play with. The children got excited about the opportunity to have a new dog, and the energy and emotional connections started building stronger than ever. Refining the details in the asking process became key as well as updating our vision board and affirmations.

The following day my husband came in from work and mentioned a man suggested we put an advertisement in the newspaper. That week we did exactly that: 'Detached House Wanted to Buy'. Two weeks later we were actually living in our new home, and it was a miracle.

We could never have planned or orchestrated this by ourselves. The universe understood our request and, of course, had our backs as we took serious action towards our intentions. A lady was very keen to sell a property that she was renting. In fact, she wanted to do it yesterday! We bought the house for cash at a lower price than previously offered, negotiated with the owner, and rang our solicitor. The paperwork was drawn up, everyone was happy, and we moved in immediately. I believe in miracles. Get out of your way and lock in to your goals. Focus only on the direction of your goals. Do not look left, do not look right. Obsess about the details of what it is you desire. Remember, it can be easy and simple.

May I add one more manifestation to this story? A month after moving into our new home, my husband tagged me in a post on social media.

A lady was relocating and needed to rehome her two adorable beagles. We expressed an interest, and she paid us a visit. And yes, our vision was complete. What picture are you painting for you right now? I will teach and share more with you about how to get yourself on that frequency to ask, believe, and receive.

Wherever possible involve other people in your family life, those who will be affected by your goal. Get them emotionally invested in the end results of visualisation, and this will help build momentum and speed up the gestation period. In my experience, involving the children is always worthy of a good goal as they manifest in lightning speed.

A Winning Attitude

Does your running commentary align you with your heartfelt desires? Do you find yourself moaning, or are you in the habit of judging and criticising others? Perhaps you even engage in self-criticism and hear yourself say, 'I am so stupid,' or, 'I always forget.' This has got to stop. It is the most important issue to work on immediately. A stinking attitude of negativity and, 'What if it goes wrong?' will not bring us the good stuff we are yearning for; it simply draws to us what we expect—more negativity.

The Law of Vibration and Attraction

Your energy vibrations attract like energy to you. This means it is a similar energy to that of your vibration. It is believed that enlightenment has the frequency of 700+ and is the greatest expansion of energy. Joy is 540 and is expansive. Anger is 150 and falls to contraction. Do you ever notice your body language can shift to the frequency you are on? Repeat to yourself a negative word such as 'sad' and observe your body's response. Then switch to 'happy' and notice the switch in your body posture, momentum, and energy.

A difference in attitude and getting what we expect is apparent in everyday life. Two people can get the polar experience in a situation because they expect different things. One can have a great attitude and believe life supports them, and the other could be sold a story that everything always goes wrong. Remember the law of polarity? You get to choose which side of the story you give attention to, believe, and accept. That is exactly where the focus will go and grow.

One thing people love to moan about constantly is the weather. This has got to be one of the most disempowering attitudes to have because we cannot really control the weather. I love Scottish comedian Billy Connelly's perspective on weather. He says,

> I hate all those weathermen who tell you that rain is bad weather, There's no such thing as bad weather, just the wrong clothing.

My bloom girl fair weather survival kit:

- Sexy raincoat
- Wellies
- Walking shoes
- Sunglasses
- Sunscreen, lots of layers, and your favourite lipstick!

Prepare for a good Irish summer. Get your wellies on, and go splash in the puddles. You have dreams to build. We need to be in the business of spotting silver linings and rainbows, or it's all over but the crying. Make stress, feeling overwhelmed, and being too busy to take care of you, a thing of the past. Busy becomes very boring to people. Begin to affirm for the perfect car parking space, the best seat in the restaurant, and helpful people wherever you go, and watch the universe support you. Think of someone who always seems to be positive and perhaps in the flow or lands on their feet. Adopt the person's attitude and expansive frequency, and know that the better life gets, the better it gets. It really is that simple. Get on the frequency and stay there.

Our family has a campervan, and we love adventures and parking right in front of the sea. It can get a little heated between us at times as it is a small space to share. Recently we set up a family rule that we all had to adopt a winning attitude towards each other. My husband said we had to, 'Big each other up'. We set personal family standards on the language we used to communicate with each other. In support of this family goal, we embraced the phrases, 'Well done', and 'That's great.' We used them even when we were feeling frustrated or exasperated. It had a huge impact, and as a result, we found ourselves giggling at situations and lighting up more. I am not saying we are perfect; we still have the occasional family 'ding dongs', but a conscious decision to make an effort, raise awareness, and increase the positive vibes is not only contagious to us but to others in the environment around us.

There is power in a group culture to raise the frequency, expand, and attract. This works for everyone regardless of the environmental setting. This can be effectively proven in small groups, large organisations, schools, and corporations. Positive language, visuals, and nonverbal communication can all contribute to the raising of the frequency.

Make the decision today to adopt a winning attitude. Raise your awareness of your responses to situations, and practise a positive response. Otherwise, it is a bit like going to a restaurant, ordering soup and expecting a three-course meal to arrive, the universe is like a cosmic kitchen when responding to your desires.

The universe is simply responding to your vibe caused by the feeling that created it. Your vibe will attract your tribe. You cannot afford the luxury of a low vibe thought, word, or comment today if you have a dream in your heart. The company we keep is important to our growth. I once heard someone say if you are the smartest person in the room, you are in the wrong room to grow.

Negative Thoughts

I never get to park here.
The restaurant is always crowded.
Everyone is always so unfriendly.
This is a disaster.

Switching Affirmations
Thank you for the perfect car parking space.
Thank you for the perfect table.
There are helpful people wherever I go.
Everything is working out perfectly.

Bloom Girl Exercise 3

Flower of life. Complete the life satisfaction reflection for growth.

Bloom Girl Exercise 4

Vision Board

Create a vision board illustrating your goals. The universe loves detail, and it is really important that you get into the Spirit and energy of what you really desire. If you want a new house, gather clippings on your ideal design and style. Does it have a gate, driveway, garden, view, how many rooms? I prefer to create my vision board on a corkboard so I can see it every day. Include affirmations supporting you to make the switch from the obstacles and limiting beliefs to what you want. Constantly impress your goals on your subconscious mind.

Esther Hicks refers to this as the 'pivot'. Some of my students like to create vision boards on their phones with apps such as the free Hay House App. You can embed positive affirmations with it.

Summary

Remember, bloom girl:

- It is safe to ask.
- You are deserving of your desires.
- The universe responds to your vibrations and meets you there.

CHAPTER 3

Your Story Pattern

Step 2—Believe
The wound is where the light enters.

—Rumi

Story is the one thing that unites all cultures; it is the most powerful tool of connectivity. I love story. I loved literature as a student, and my first degree was in English literature. There is something magical about a great story, and it is one sure way of connecting with each other and opening the heart. As a primary-school teacher, picture books were a primary resource to me for leading the learning as they were the best way, I found to engage children. When our first child was born, our daughter Roisin, one of the first things I recall doing was visiting the bookstore and buying about twenty picture books. The pages were bursting with lively characters, colourful illustrations, rhythmic language, and humour. I had actually started reading to her when she was in the womb.

In this chapter I invite you to connect with your story because we all have one. This is an integral and pivotal point of development to ensure your growth. Within our stories lie nuggets of information and treasures that can really catapult our growth and breakthroughs. Our stories create our repeat patterns in life, self-belief systems, and paradigms.

It is the paradigm that drives our daily habits, mostly unconsciously, and produces results in our current lifestyles. Every experience is reflected to us in our day-to-day activities, work, and relationships. It is believed that 95 per cent of our decisions and responses are made in the subconscious mind, and it is also the residence of our inner child. Therefore, we can conclude that a very young version of ourselves is often directing the show and with a very old programme. When we step into our stories and feel their enormity, only then can we experience freedom and stop dancing to everyone else's drumbeat. We arrive at the destination of knowing and have nothing to prove to the outside world. Just like the trees and the flowers, we no longer have to worry or hurry. We have no extra baggage to lug around. The contrast is one huge shift from heavy to light and emptying ourselves of guilt and shame. The guilty belief one often holds of, 'I made a mistake', or the shame of, 'I am a mistake.' The reality is we all got it wrong at some point, and it's time to let it go.

In the classroom, getting children to write was often a sticky wicket, and I frequently sought inspirational resources. I particularly embraced the work of Pie Corbett, who encouraged story maps. We would simply draw a squiggly line and invite each child to create a story. The line represented the stages in the story. They were drawn from the top to the bottom of the page, representing the beginning, middle, and end. The children could illustrate the story using symbols, drawings, sounds, words, any representations they could get down on paper in any form. I adapted this resource to use in my coaching work and workshops to support clients in expressing their own personal stories and memories. It is time to take your little girl on a journey and join a few dots while looking back.

As children we are like little sponges; we soak up everything in our environments. We are completely susceptible and accept and believe everything as truth. We are influenced by family, community, clergy, and school. Authority figures have a huge impact on the belief system that we create about ourselves. It is thought that by the age of about 7 years old we have created the self-image handed to us and accept it as our truth. If the story is one with trauma and emotional pain, we can then unconsciously live life from the place of the wound. Woundology can consume us and become our identities. This can be very far removed from the perfection of the new-born incarnated as explored in chapter 1—perfect, whole, and complete. Bring your attention to the image or experience you can recall of a new born—the whites of a baby's eyes, the pureness of the baby's skin, and the absolute beauty of the divine light shining from within. This light somehow gets dimmed and contaminated by the outside environment and social systems.

These negative belief systems are usually not in alignment with our true natures. They can be ancestral, going back as far as five or even seven generations. Deepak Chopra, in a conversation with the mystic Sadhguru, refers to an experiment carried out on mice. He claims that mice were taken, offered some wintergreen, and sent mild electric shocks. They came to associate the wintergreen with pain and danger. And not only did these mice carry this fear, it was traced down the next seven generations. Science is opening the window to what the Eastern tradition has always known—we are more than the body. It is time to get more curious about the invisible world or just accept that our essential being is greater than the material world. We simply inherit our ancestors' stuff unless we courageously wake up and willingly and consciously clear it. The point of this reflection is not to impose blame or carry resentment but to remember everyone was doing their best with the understanding they had at that time, and chances are they did not know any better. They were simply operating with the manual and programme that was modelled and handed down to them.

We can now undo any of the beliefs that no longer serve us, thereby changing and shifting the patterns and raising our consciousnesses. This empowers us to create new daily habits and thought patterns, change our results to beautiful mindsets, and manifest our goals of abundance and prosperity. We want to plant our seeds of desire in the richest fertile soil. In weeding out our inner garden, we are guaranteed to bloom and flourish.

The flower of life categories is again very useful here to begin to explore what you have learnt, absorbed, and accepted as your truth when growing up. What did you see and learn to develop the beliefs you have about relationships, money, gender, sexuality, and the role of women? Create a story map using the downloadable at www.catrionajones. com/bloomgirl. Go back as far as you can remember in chronological order. At the beginning of the map list any memories, sayings, and experiences, and gently build on the story. When you spot it, you got it! Awareness is the key to bringing the beliefs and programming that no longer serve you to light. On this journey we must be prepared to let go and walk away from any beliefs, people, situations, and environments that no longer serve our purposes and visions that we have for ourselves. What is getting in the way of you blooming today?

Let me illustrate with an example of how story affects our social beliefs. One of the workshops I teach is exploring your money blocks in my Money Mindset Coaching programme which supports women in clearing their money blocks and receive abundance. Our money story can be one of the most loaded topics in society. It's up there with sex and often regarded the 'dirty bit' at the end of a transaction. What did your parents or caregivers believe about money? What were their experiences? This is the point of facilitation in a group. We might start to discuss and share expressions and sayings such as, 'Money is the root of all evil', 'Money is corrupt', and 'There's no money in a shroud.' If we experienced a lack of money and scarcity of prosperity growing up, we can have a huge paradigm to shift. This is so far from the actual truth. It is natural to desire more money for expansion and to be the best versions of ourselves by enjoying everything that is available to us and nurturing the whole of ourselves in mind, body, and spirit, no component left behind. It can take time to accept and realign with the truth that abundance is indeed our birthright. But we can do it!

Exploring our personal journeys can connect us deeper with the belief system that dictates current results. Your current world reflects everything you believe about yourself and your deservability. Self-image is a huge piece in the world of healing and growing. We can only achieve and stretch as far as the beliefs we hold about ourselves. I remember very vividly the early days of my journey with self-image. I held some beliefs that really did not serve me at all, including a core belief that I was ugly. Today I believe that every single human being is beautiful, and beauty takes so many forms—from the way someone might smile, adjust himself or herself, or tilt one's head. Every one of us is a work of art in our appearance, expressions, mannerisms, and poise.

Learning to love and approve of ourselves is the most beautiful gift that we can give ourselves and loved ones around us, particularly our children. We set them free from any ancestral self-doubt. On reflection, my early journey was very much one of self-doubt and approval seeking. I was striving for perfection and eventually wore myself out hiding behind the mask of superwoman. I often struggled to find love because I lacked self-love and self-approval. My personal story took a turn for the best when I was a young mother, although it did not feel like that at the time.

My Story

My husband and I lived in Wales. We had a very comfortable lifestyle with our own home, travel, a connection to nature, and good friendships. I did not always have a permanent teaching post, and although this frustrated me, I was never out of work. We were newly married after a number of years backpacking the world, and it would be fair to say we were both ready to settle. Now that I had the beautiful country cottage in the valleys, the loyal supportive husband, my soulmate, we were keen to start a family. This all sounds like a simple process, but it took some time to manifest. When I look back on my life, my beliefs around worthiness always took a toll on one area of my life.

If work and money would flow, I would lack romance. If romance was working out, my mind would slip to weight management and body image, work unrest or staff politics. The greedy mind would always find fault and give me a piece to obsess about and to remind me that I was not up to the mark. My low self-worth and negative self-image exhausted me by making me believe that there was always something within me that needed fixed. This manifested as daily anxiety and later on through IBS. I was intense, confrontational, and unsettled within. The 'fighting Irish' in me was clearly activated but not in the most loving passionate way! Somewhere within was the belief that I couldn't have balance, that I had to settle in one particular area. My worthiness got in the way of enjoying a healthy and balanced life.

My lack of self-belief, self-approval held in my inner world was reflected in my outer world. I regularly found myself at the centre of disharmony, inequality, and bullying situations. It would play out as feeling exiled from community, not accepted within circles, and a victim to group hatred. I choose to wear this victim badge with honour. I walked into these situations repeatedly and played the role willingly. Drama and chaos will repeatedly show itself in our lives until we do the inner work and clean up our energy fields. Then we begin to think more highly of ourselves. We remain magnets for dysfunction until we clear up this low energy. The dark shadows of the victim and the martyr do not serve our highest good to or for all.

My anxiety intensified, manifested in my judgement and blaming of others for my unfair and 'imperfect' life until I experienced a miscarriage of our first baby. It was our worst nightmare come true, and we were both heartbroken. I once again slipped into self-blame. I knew I had to seek support and managed to rejoin a self-help circle that I was familiar with from the past and got support for myself. The words of the midwife at that time rang true to form, and I was pregnant again by our original due date.

It often takes a painful experience to drive us to embrace healing and change. The ego wants to hold on to the pain, and we believe holding on makes us strong. I once heard it perfectly described as like wearing armour but with the spikes on the inside. There are perfect psychological reasons why we hold on to hurtful experiences, negative thinking patterns of 'I'm not good enough', and the suspicion and judgement of others. The egotistical mind wants to protect us from potential danger and keep us safe. It is the job of the mind to activate our fight, flight, or freeze instinct and protect us. Our minds have gone on high alert about everything, believing that if someone takes our car parking spaces, it is life threatening. This low vibrational energy will persist in our lives until we suffer too much emotionally, and the price becomes too high to our emotional well-being. We then make a conscious decision to tame the mind, quiet that chimp or 'monkey on the back', and rationalise the crazy thinking and critical voice. We learn to master our thoughts and emotions and to respond as opposed to react. Don't let other people's behaviours dictate how you behave in the world.

As I began to relax a little with life and surround myself with positive support and self-help books, letting go of self-sabotage, we were blessed with a beautiful daughter. A perfect wee rosebud weighing only five pounds seven ounces, and she just took our breath away. I recall my husband telling me that he had never seen me laugh or smile so much as following her birth. A daughter, a wee girl to love and cherish. And little did I know she would show me the way to deeper inner healing. Each stage of her development would create an opportunity to invite my inner child out to play and reflect to me any stages of my development that required soothing and nurturing. As mothers, we have responsibilities to our children—and to our daughters particularly—to become great role models, so we can continue to be a leading force in the dismantling of patriarchy in the world. I was committed to this journey and willing to do whatever it would take to forge this path even more and lay the tracks for her and all the women to follow me. We must move beyond pretty and teach them to really *know* they are smart, creative, analytical, resourceful, problem-solvers, strong, and courageous.

Roisin was easy-going in nature, and motherhood came naturally to me. I loved every moment and cherished every wee burp, fart, and smile. I was a little put out when the animated elderly lady with glasses down the street stole her first smile! I loved being a mammy and was thrilled to be expecting baby two not long after! The pregnancy was healthy again, thank God, and the bump was bigger! Labouring with Ioan, our son, was not so quick and straightforward. It was long and would stop and start. I became exhausted and was admitted to hospital, saying farewell to my planned home birth and risking a section. Determined to deliver myself, I recall the moments before Ioan's birth very vividly. I was vulnerable, exhausted, and worn out, I reached for my husband's hand, and weeping begged, 'Don't leave me. Please don't ever leave me.'

My fear of abandonment crept right up and out and into the light. Half an hour later, Ioan was born; a natural birth delivery, of course, out of sheer determination to do my best and delivery myself. Natural birth is great, and recovery is easier. But today I also admire women who give themselves permission to opt for surgery during a long labour and not put unnecessary pressure on themselves. There is strength and courage in every decision we make as women.

Ioan was an enthusiastic, formidable redhead, and our family felt complete. I had everything I ever dreamed of, the loving husband, beautiful healthy children, a safe home. Everything intact but my worthiness. There was no energy left to paper over the cracks and wear the mask of superwoman. Six months later I hit my rock bottom. And then, my lovelies, I truly began to unfold and bloom.

I vividly remember my midwife telling me, 'Now, Catriona, when you are in labour, it will come to a point when you might actually say, "I can't do this anymore." We, your midwives, will be rallying around because we know then at that point your baby is coming.' I love that memory, the process in birthing. Just when we feel we can't do it anymore—new life! It is not unusual that when the going gets tough in life and on the goal achievement path, we sometimes opt out just as the shoots are about to appear. Never give up on your dreams. Know you will manifest, birth, and create. We must push through that resistance, the pain threshold, and know you are at nine centimetres. Women usually birth at 10 centimetres. Look to nature, and as Rumi said, 'the crack is where the light shines through.' Set yourself a command and follow it.

How often have you given up on your dreams? It is like the tragic story of the man who stopped digging only to find out later he was three feet from gold.

When the student is ready, the teacher will appear. I loved motherhood, gave everything to family life, and have totally embraced my healing. The only way is up, and I am now holding on to the belief that I have a place in the world, and my husband and children do need me.

I was shopping in town and briskly manoeuvring my way through the busy shoppers with my double buggy, headed in the direction of the bookstore. Books are always a go-to for me to quench my constant thirst to study and learn more. I walk to the self-help section, and as I reached for a book, another book landed in my hands: *You Can Heal Your Life* by Louise Hay. The word 'heal' made me slightly uncomfortable, but the ego is quiet as I have now surrendered and admitted I cannot do this journey on my own. It is okay to ask for help. I bought the book and am delighted to have something to read for the weekend. We go away in our touring caravan, and I devoured the book. I am inspired. Tears flowed—tears of relief and joy, excitement and hope. What an amazing woman. Louise Hay takes all our excuses away. This book changed my life, and following this awakening, I signed up to become a life coach. My mind totally expanded to new possibilities. I was grounded and centred. A spark ignited in me from a place of darkness; it had never been activated so powerfully before. *Brace yourself, world,* I thought. *I am coming in for a landing!* I had experienced a significant quantum leap in my journey, and it felt so good.

If you take one thing only from my story, may it be this: You are never alone with your thoughts in the world. Others have shared those same thoughts, low times too. And even though your experience is unique to you, others have experienced similar emotional pain and broken through. A thought is just a thought, and you can change a thought in a second. You can do this and turn your life around. And most important of all, you are worthy and loveable. I hold your beautiful heart as you read this book and prepare to bloom fully for the world. Take the first step: Let go and trust. Have the courage to invest time with a counsellor, therapist, or trusted friend and tell your story. Gently peel the layers of the onion in a safe space; share and express how you feel. Our powers are revealed in our vulnerabilities. Power comes from the deep, dark soil that the seeds manifest in and come to bloom. I love what Brené Brown teaches. She says that shame is the most powerful master emotion. It is consumed with the fear that we are not good enough. Shame cannot survive when it is spoken about in the presence of an empathetic ear.

> Shame needs three things to grow secrecy, silence and judgement. (Brené Brown)

Take that little girl by the hand, and show her the way home to non-judgemental and pure unconditional love. She has been waiting for a very long time. It is time and safe to open up.

Mind–Body Connection

It is safe to feel, express, and release. As I began to transition out of teaching in the traditional sense, I found I loved my work as a life coach and image consultant. I became aware of an inner piece of work that my clients often needed. It was the exact set of tools that I had read about in Louise Hay's bestselling book *You Can Heal Your Life*. I trained and became a Heal Your Life Workshop teacher and coach under the gentle guidance and direction of Patricia Crane, Heart Inspired. I attended global training with students worldwide. The wonderful energy and the process shared was the icing on the cake to not only my own personal journey but in my service to my clients also. I had a full week in the wonderful energy of Patricia, her husband, Rick, and the amazing group to identify my limiting beliefs, let go, heal my past, and embrace the future. It was an inner journey of self-love which was to change my entire life and the way I viewed the world. We spent time punching pillows to release anger, pushing through resistance, dissolving resentment, dancing to celebrate our inner children, and reflecting to forgive and let go.

When my husband and children collected me on my return at the airport, I hugged them in a way that I had never opened myself up to before. I felt light and free, beautiful and alive. My husband held me that night and told me that when I arrived at the airport, I looked like a queen. The wound was healing, and I will treasure that shift all my life.

The old limiting beliefs I held were dissolving, and as I continued to use the tools every day, I bloomed more and more. My heart is truly grateful to Patricia Crane and all the beautiful souls in the group who held space for me that week and reminded me every single day—sometimes every hour—the truth about how beautiful I really am. The process of connecting to my body was a simple one but not easy. I am honoured to share this beautiful process with women all over the world today. Patricia and Rick continue to teach this wonderful work globally at www.heartinspired.com.

> Both the good in our lives and the dis-ease are the results of mental thought patterns that form our experiences. We all have thought patterns that produce good, positive experiences, and these we enjoy. It's the negative thought patterns that produce uncomfortable, unrewarding experiences with which we are concerned. It's our desire to change dis-ease in life into perfect health. (Louise Hay)

In my personal transformation, it was sheer joy to experience metaphysical causations and witness my opening up and blooming that week. These tools work when we work them.

The aches, pains, and sensations in our bodies often reflect our mental and emotional patterns we experience inside. If we get in touch and listen to our bodies, we can intuitively connect with this physical pain. My body never lets me down and continues to give me wonderful feedback. It is safe to feel what is going on in your body, connect with the emotion, express it, and then release it and let it go.

My Client Maureen

Maureen came to me heartbroken and said, 'I just can't stop crying.' She had given up on life. She thought she was happily married until she discovered that her husband, who had been drinking too much, had betrayed their marriage. He left her for another woman, and she just could not get over this emotional pain and mistrust. I listened to

Maureen tell her story and held a sacred space for her hurt and tender heart as she entered the healing process.

As she began to open up and get honest about her feelings, I encouraged Maureen to connect with her body and the little girl within. It was hard at first because she felt her inner child was very afraid and hiding. However, as soon as Maureen invited her into her open arms, as you would any frightened little girl, it opened the gates to healing. Maureen's whole countenance changed, and her heart opened too. She reassured her inner child and reconnected with her fun and creative energy. Keeping her safe, hope returned, and Maureen welcomed joy back into her life. In the months following, she experienced a burst of energy and trust returned.

Maureen was in awe of what her body communicated to her and the magic that the inner child connection and healing brought her; she did not take her eyes off her inner child. She was able to forgive her ex-husband and shared gratitude that the break happened exactly when it did. Life for her just got better and better. Maureen travelled and opened her own business.

In building personal self-worth and working on self-image with my clients, the third chakra is often activated, blocked, or unsettled, representing our confidence, self-worth, and worthiness in the world. When nurturing and healing our inner children, I find the following archetypes from Caroline Myss helpful.

Inner Child Archetypes

Child Magical—Sees potential for sacred beauty in all things, gifted with imagination and belief all things are possible. Healing helps to overcome lack of faith in miracles and transformation.

Child Nature—Inspires connection and bonding with all life, humans, nature, and animals with inner toughness and an ability to survive. Healing involves overcoming a tendency to abuse people, animals, and the environment.

Child Orphan—Reflects feelings that you are not part of your family or tribal spirit. Healing will overcome immaturity and searching to belong to a group or tribe.

Child Wounded—Holds memories of abuse, neglect, and other traumas. Healing will overcome the habit of blame, self-pity, and resistance, moving through to forgiveness.

Bloom Girl Exercise 5

What negative message can you remember being told growing up? Expect the energy to dip a little during this exercise, but it is important to name it, feel it, express it, and then release it.

What negative message does your inner child still believe about herself?

How does your inner teenager feel?

Collate photographs and connect deeper with these parts of you. Please seek support to honour your healing journey. You are deserving of this breakthrough and shift.

Bloom Girl Exercise 6

Complete inner child story map.

Write a love letter to your inner child.

What does your inner child yearn to hear today or maybe every day?

Remember to embed these soothing affirmations:

I am safe in the world.

It is safe for me to feel, express, and release.

I am worthy.

I am enough.

I approve of myself.

It is safe for me to embrace my healing journey.

Today I honour my inner child.

My inner teenager trusts me and knows I approve of her.

Summary

Remember, bloom girl:

- It is safe to feel, express, and release.
- You are deserving of a beautiful life.
- A thought is just a thought, and you can turn that thought around.

You can download my inner child guided meditation at www. catrionajones.com/bloomgirl.

CHAPTER 4

I Am Oh So Zen Now

Step 3—Receive
Calmness of mind is one of the
beautiful jewels of wisdom.
—James Allen, *As a Man Thinketh,* 1902

You are meant to bloom and be a wonderful expression of the divine. The infinite intelligence is within each of us, that place where our perfect DNA resides. The power is within, and life is waiting for you to open up to it more. We have more understanding today about all the components of who we really are. We know we are more than the body and the mind. We are pure energy and have a spiritual essence within that is ours to tap into, claim, and express. This deeper space in each of us is unlimited and free of self-doubt, fear, judgement, and criticism. We access this field of pure potentiality through silence. I treasure the silent moments in my life today because I know in this stillness there is a state of pure potential for the sacred to unfold and connect me to truth and my purpose on this earth. God doesn't make an excess of anything nor create mistakes; everything created by God has a divine purpose and meaning for life.

A great self-development program will nurture and nourish all parts of you, including the mind, body, and soul supporting your physical, mental, emotional, and spiritual well-being. In order to expand and build greater self-belief, we need to develop and build our spiritual muscles. It can sometimes feel hard to grasp that in slowing down we become more productive. There is no quick fix or spiritual bypass. This inner work is essential through the practice of mediation and daily spiritual rituals. These tools are at the core of my Zen coaching program, and the calmness of my mind has become my greatest power. I have spent many years overthinking and lying awake at night, regurgitating old thoughts and conversations from the day. Before I would hold on to what other people thought and complain and blame. This is very disempowering and results in beginning your day already running on empty. These tools offer practical and mainstream techniques to empower you to flourish and bloom from a place of love and peace, understanding the connection of presence and power, and consciously choosing to shift from the victim or saboteur archetype to reclaiming your personal feminine power.

My Zen coaching tools offer you the opportunity to journey within and create a more beautiful life. In this chapter I guide you and support your spiritual development and support you in quieting the mind and organising all four structures and dimensions within you—body, mind, emotions, and Spirit—and keep yourself in congruence with divine order. You can have daily habits and rituals to support your growth and raise your frequency to align with and prepare to receive your goals. You see, everything is energy and frequency, and we can only attract that which is on our same frequency levels. If we are stressed out and embedded in a chaotic lifestyle, then we are operating at a low-level frequency. We are also affected by the environment and people around us. Everyone, everything, and every place holds energy and operates on a frequency. These tools raise your frequency and protect your energy.

However, it is up to you to become more aware and to eliminate any low-level energy that is affecting your vibration and attraction, taking full responsibility for change required and personal growth. This can involve processing and alkalising our own pain body and density we might be holding on to and carrying. In effect, taking full responsibility for the energy we carry and bring into a space and world around us. So many people live or merely exist from a place of fear in the world. It is time to pivot and raise up humanity.

The benefits of meditation are well researched and documented. Everything that happens in the mind has a physical imprint or representation in the body. Everything that happens in the brain is in direct correlation with what is happening in the body. Therefore, our perceptions of everyday life, memories from the past, and all emotions past or present influence and affect the body. This is the heart of the personal relationship of the mind, spirit, and body, an intricately woven process. When we organise these dimensions in one direction, we become unwavering from our lives' purpose, goals, and desires. We live a life of flow, fully connected to ourselves and each other. Imagine, if we taught this in schools the power that our children would harness. The Dalai Lama claims if every 8-year-old in the world is taught meditation, we will eliminate violence from the world in one generation.

Negative experiences and emotions cause toxicity in the body. And stored over a period of time, they cause discomfort, disease, and illness. The practice of meditation raises our awareness of any disharmony within the body and can detoxify these foreign elements. Scientific research now concludes that the practice of meditation will bring the body back to its natural state of homeostasis, creating a balance in hormones, the digestive system, boosting the immune system, and therefore, going into self-repair and self-healing at a deep cellular level. We can lower cortisol levels that are associated with stress and low mood and boost dopamine, serotonin, and oxytocin without medication.

There is a significant increase in the number of people suffering from overwhelm, stress, anxiety, and depression in the world today. Work-related stress has become very apparent, and I share these exact techniques with organisations, corporations, and schools. Although the recommendation is to practice stillness daily, I have worked with companies and employees that claim to have experienced less stress from one thirty-minute lunchtime meditation class a week. Employees reported noticing increased productivity, feeling increasingly more relaxed, having additional energy, and experiencing more fun and light-heartedness in the workplace. Companies that invest in Zen coaching and the well-being of their employees benefit from the increased focus, productivity, and less illness from work. The small financial investment will easily outweigh the financial savings on the illness-related pay budget.

Whatever reservations or preconceived judgements you might have regarding the practice of meditation or contemplation and to which religion or traditions it belongs with, I encourage you to be open to this practice. I am by no means suggesting you dishonour your personal religious or spiritual beliefs. Nor do I recommend ignoring valuable medical advice for your health challenges. However, if you have not tried this practice to compliment your well-being regime, reduce stress, and promote better health, I recommend you give it a go.

Embedding more Zen into your daily lifestyle will have so many other benefits. I find it boosts my creativity, clarity, and focus. In my work I love to use the analogy of becoming an emotional banker. If we were to monitor how we use our energy and emotions as carefully as our money, we could all be emotional millionaires and raise the bank balance in the process. We would rarely walk into a store or shop and purchase items that we didn't wholeheartedly approve of and desire. In fact, I put careful thought into choosing furniture for our home and clothes I wear. Yet we throw away our emotional energy almost every day when we give energy to negative comments by others and behaviours of work colleagues or family. I compare this to walking down the street and throwing money down the drain, a complete and utter waste. The practice of meditation reduces distraction, quieting the overthinking mind and decreasing negative thought patterns.

Everyone is on their own journeys, and attitudes and behaviour towards you reflect their inside wounds or pains. It is not personal, and chances are they treat others in that way too. Ask yourself, if my energy were money, how much of it would I invest in that thought, comment, or feedback right now? It is time to stop being so free with our energies and power in other people's stuff. Our job is to reserve and conserve our energies and perhaps even live off our interests. Imagine living a high-energy life like that? The tools I am about to share with you will top up your emotional energy bank every day.

Eckhart Tolle is one of the great masters on spiritual enlightenment and the profound wisdom to be found in stillness. Falling still and meditating will uncover the hidden depths of your ability and full potential. In *Stillness Speaks,* Tolle claims,

> The transformation of human consciousness is no longer a luxury, so to speak, available only to a few isolated individuals, but a necessity if humankind is not to destroy itself.

Being more Zen, embracing relaxation, and downtime are being globally recognised and appreciated in the corporate world. It is no longer regarded that there is a certain cultural group that appreciates nature and yoga. The stigma is lifting, and we are waking up. Robin Sharma, a globally respected leadership and personal optimisation adviser, had this to say recently:

> Relaxation and rest can peak performance. Enables it. You can't perform at dominant levels without being relaxed, rested, fresh and happy. And what I am going to suggest to you is this: Work less and you'll succeed more. The most effective geniuses, scientists, the great geniuses were amazing at having fun, resting, recovering and relaxing.

The Bloom Girl Zen Toolkit

Create a Zen Space

The first thing I always recommend to clients is to create a Zen space, your own sacred space that you associate with relaxation and reflection. Your home and work environments can affect your mood. Research studies reveal that beautiful surroundings can have a positive impact on our energies. Choose a defined place at home where you can sit comfortably to reflect. Create a Zen space for *you*. These techniques are also useful for workspaces, particularly when providing a self-development or holistic therapy service for others. Consider how it will positively impact your self-care.

Cleansing Your Space

Everything is energy, and when working with energy, we have to set intention and give a command. The following is a prayer I love to use to cleanse a space and create a clean, crisp environment free from negative energy. You are welcome to use it if it appeals to you. Remember there is no right or wrong in the language or choice of words. Just keep the intention pure and instruction clear.

Zen-Clearing Preparation

Using and burning white sage, move in a clockwise direction following the outline of the floor area of the space you want to cleanse. In a small room, this could simply be a movement from corner to corner. In a larger open plane, you can simply map the area out in your mind's eye or mark the boundaries with four crystals acting as corners. Pyrite or clear quartz crystals are my favourites for this cleansing process, and they will help seal the energy of your cleansed space. I often situate four crystals on my workspace, too, to raise the vibration and seal the energy. Always remember to connect within and be guided from your inner compass and wisdom. These are merely suggestions for support.

The Clearing and Cleansing Prayer
Heavenly Father,
Cleanse and clear any negative energy from this space now.
Return it with love to its Source clean. (Repeat three times.)
Mother Earth,
Fill this space with love, light, and peace. (Repeat three times.)

Personalise your space with your essence. Objects might include comfortable cushions, soft furnishings, flowers or greenery, crystals, special objects, photos, candles, incense, diffusers, essential oils, reflective literature/books, journal/notebook and inspirational quotes.

Marie Kondo has shared the most delightful gift with the world in her work *The Life Changing Magic of Tidying Up*. She offers the simplest tools in an attempt to empower people to spark more joy. Your home and workspace are reflections of your energy. Decluttering is a great way of letting go of the past as 'stuff' holds energy, particularly other people's stuff, whether it is a painting, book, or craft. Unless I totally love it, I bless it and pass it on with love. I have to be completely honest with you. I can experience total contentment about an orderly sock drawer, just saying.

Evidence supports the theory that we have our strongest wills and are more alert in the morning. This is the best time to invest in our energies and to get on the frequency for the day. Set yourself up for success with a sound foundation of good, solid morning rituals. I recommend that you choose at least five daily habits to complete before 9 a.m. The earlier you rise in the morning the better. For optimal effect, it is suggested that we synchronise our beings with nature and get up with the sun. That is optional, of course. May I suggest you intentionally start by setting your alarm thirty minutes earlier than usual and just do it. The congruence you will experience with all four structures within you is so powerful.

I love to wake early in the morning to the sound of the birds while the children are still asleep, and I have the first few hours of the day to set myself up. This helps create a sense of calm and positive energy in our home at the beginning of each new day. I relax in my sacred Zen space and begin with a pause, connecting to my body and the senses. Then I meditate. The body is always in the present and will bring us into the now. Regular meditation empowers me to be more mindful throughout the day.

People often ask me the question what the difference is between mindfulness and meditation. Meditation for me is the actual practice of sitting still and developing the skill of being aware of thought and staying consciously present in the moment. It helps train my mind to focus and be present. Mindfulness is the result of my meditation practice. It helps me to stay present throughout the day. Let me share an example with you. I have learnt to focus continuously on bringing my attention only to the task at hand. If I am washing my hands, I connect to my senses and sensations experienced to be fully present, optimising the performance of every action I take to the best possible outcome. I feel the water, I smell the soap, I observe the movement of my hands, I hear the running water, and enjoy the touch and sensation of the water and soap lather. This will empower you to increase your focus and attention in all areas of your day and life. To show up alert and focussed. As I notice my attention beginning to falter and my mind increasingly wandering, I press pause again, bringing my attention to the present moment and the task in hand.

These techniques are the starting points that I introduce for learning to meditate and embed mindfulness into your daily life. If you want to know where to start, begin here with your breath. Paying attention to the breath will bring you into your body and the present moment.

Three Deep, Clearing Breaths

Breath is life itself, and as long as we breathe, we live in this world. The practice of focusing on your breathing as a way to calm the body and performing a series of breathing exercises can immediately shift your energy emotionally and physically. When we breathe in, we can potentially live in the present, the here and now, and exhale the past. I love taking three deep, clearing breaths before any of my morning rituals or daily spiritual Zen tools outlined in this chapter. Just like meditation, yoga, and breath work, there are many great techniques. I choose to keep it simple, and this works for me, my clients, and in my workshops.

Apparently when we are born, we naturally breathe deeply from the belly. And as we grow, as young as starting school, and experience stress, we shorten our breaths and breathe from the chest area.

Sit comfortably on a chair. Rest your feet on the ground, and relax your shoulders. Breathe in deeply through your nose. Take in as much air as you comfortably can for the count of four. Then release it through the mouth. Really focus on emptying your lungs. Many people hold air in their lungs after an exhale, so emptying your lungs on a deep exhale can help you to get more fresh oxygen into them. Exhale to the count of six. Making the exhale longer can help empty the lungs.

Breathe in deeply through the nose for four seconds.

Exhale completely through the mouth for six seconds (three times).

The three deep breaths can be applied at any time through relaxation and meditation to continue regulating your breathing, reducing anxiety until you find your own natural rhythm.

Sitting Position and the Chakra System

Sitting in an upright position is recommended for energy clearing as the chakra system, one's energy system and where the spirit manifests within the body, is structured through the central core axis from the crown of the head to the base of the spine. Sitting upright when possible, will optimise the relaxation experience, allowing the energy of the body to flow.

Each person's unique energy field draws energy from source, the universe, our life force. This energy is drawn into the body via each of the chakras. If the chakras are blocked or there is a kink in the hose so to speak, the energy will not flow, causing a blockage. Although anatomically undetectable and somewhat invisible, the seven major chakras are linked with our physical and emotional well-being. I have devised this table based on the ancient cultures of the East, now being accepted in the West, to help assist your understanding of the physical and emotional correlation and association of each of the seven chakras. The old paradigm of relating to health as purely visible is now disappearing, and a deeper appreciation of the invisible energy system is growing, an acceptance of our nonphysical components. In meditation we come to know ourselves deeper. Then we can show up as the best versions of our true selves and serve others in the world.

Chakra Well-Being

Chakra	Location	Colour and Element	Association	Physical Connection	Crystal	Healing Process and Affirmation
1 Root	Base of spine	Red Earth Grounded	Tribal beliefs Power, sex, and money Fight, flight, or freeze	Adrenal glands	Red jasper Bija mantra Lam	Releasing frustration, tribal guilt. Allows manifestations. I am grounded, and centred, and it is safe for me to honour my purpose.
2 Sacral	Lower belly	Orange Water In flow	Personal relationship with sexuality, sensuality, and creativity.	Ovaries and testes	Carnelian Bija mantra Vam	Releases anger. Allows creative flow and pleasure. I feel safe and connected to my power within.
3 Solar Plexus	Belly (above the belly button)	Yellow Fire Self-mastery	Self-esteem and self-worth	Stomach, kidneys, liver	Yellow calcite Bija mantra Ram	Releases fear and anxiety. Enhances energy, confidence, and courage. I do good in the world with confidence and courage.
4 Heart	Above the heart (Bridge between earth and Spirit)	Green Air Love	Love and compassion	Thymus gland, immune system	Green adventurine Bija mantra Yam	Releases apathy, allows love. I love and approve of myself and others

5 Throat	Throat	Blue Ether/Space Purification	Expression and communication	Parathyroid glands	Sodalite Bija mantra Ham	Releases misunderstanding. Allows clear communication. I speak my truth with love and grace.
6 Third Eye	Between the eyebrows	Indigo Light Mind	Intuition and Vision (sixth sense)	Pituitary gland	Amethyst Bija mantra OM	Releases confusion/ignorance. Allows knowledge and true will. I see clearly now from a place of calm and trust.
7 Crown	Top of head	Violet-white All that is Thought/Cosmos	Clarity, wisdom, and higher states of consciousness	Pineal gland	Clear quartz Bija mantra Silence (we just listen)	Releases obsession. Allows calm and divine guidance. I know and understand that I am divinely guided and have a soul purpose on earth.

Chakra Healing

When you place the crystal on the energy point, you will get a sense of it settling and connecting. Connect intuitively with your crystals and relax. Rest with the crystal on your chakras for ten to twenty minutes. You will get a sense of when the crystals have completed their work.

Chakra Healing Affirmations

1. I am grounded and centred, and it is safe for me to honour my purpose.
2. I feel safe and connected to my power within.
3. I do well in the world with confidence and courage.
4. I love and approve of myself and others.
5. I speak my truth with love and grace.
6. I see clearly now from a place of calm and trust.
7. I know and understand that I am divinely guided and have a soul purpose on earth.

Press Pause

Sitting in an upright position, back straight, two feet on the ground, and relax your shoulders.

Take three deep, clearing breaths.

Keep two feet flat on the ground, body uncrossed, and connect with your body.

Ensure your chin is parallel to the floor.

Gently close your eyes, and allow your breath to find its own natural rhythm.

Connect with your sense of hearing. What sounds do you hear? Connect with your sense of smell. What fragrances do you smell? Connect with your sense of taste. What can you taste? Sometimes we can taste the trace of coffee or tea on the tongue. Connect with your sense of touch and the play of air on your skin or touch of clothing, the feel of your hands resting on your lap.

As you connect to all of your senses and experience a deeper sense of relaxation you can either repeat the word 'Peace' quietly and inwardly to yourself, or the affirmation 'I am Calm' or the mantra So Hum.

I use all these separately in my relaxation, sometimes just a word, a fitting affirmation or the mantra. 'So hum' is derived from Sanskrit and literally means, 'I am that.' It means identifying oneself with the universe or ultimate reality. As we relax or meditate on this, we realise that we are all one, an extension of consciousness. There is a beautiful connectedness experienced in chatting this mantra.

I recall a period in my life prior to learning to meditate. You may remember I mentioned backpacking with my husband (then boyfriend) around Asia. My anxiety had intensified, and my mind was on overdrive with thoughts and stories. We were visiting the majestic Angkor Wats, a temple complex in Cambodia.

Built in the first half of the twelfth century, it is one of the largest religious monuments in the world. We spent days exploring the grounds. One morning I observed a group of Buddhist nuns meditating. It was so peaceful and surreal. I have a photograph of me watching them, and I look puzzled and mesmerised at the same time. I felt a deep yearning to experience what they had accessed. It was a snippet of heaven, and I felt frustrated that they didn't speak English, I wanted them to teach me there and then, give me the quick fix.

Following that experience I began to practise pausing, but I had no system as such, no mobile phone or social media to assist me. However, a knowing within me was awakened, a knowing that there is a place of peace within. I had observed it, but more important, I felt it. Amid all my anxiety and my chaotic mind, I experienced the nonphysical part of the human being.

Learning to meditate takes time, and I devoted to this journey of stillness and peace observed at the Angkor Wats and inspired by our travels in the Far East. I can wholeheartedly claim and reassure you that if I can learn to meditate, so can you. Clients often say to me, 'I can't meditate. Every time I try to sit still, I have lots of thoughts.' My response is always reassurance that, that's it. You are meditating because you are becoming aware and connected to your thoughts. Just observe them as if clouds passing in the sky. The thoughts lessen and the gap between thoughts and silence widen, but don't judge it. Accept each experience as unique, and it is what it is. Just as the heart has a job to keep beating, the mind's job is to think. It takes commitment and daily practice.

Throughout my meditation practice, I have come to experience the most beautiful sense of inner peace and a constant reminder that I am safe in the world. Life loves me and moves through and for me. The universe is on my side and has always been in my corner. This rule of discovery applies to you, too, my lovely. You have got this journey, and everything is going to be better than okay. Be still, and remember you are pure light and peace within. Anxiety and depression can be overcome. Hold on to this: If she can do it, so can I. Inner peace is the new success story. All roads to an elite performance and success in all areas of life flow from this sweet spot.

As you practise and develop the pause you will naturally expand into longer periods of stillness and learn to meditate. Let go of judgement. Simply set the intention in your mind and heart to pause and be still. Begin to pause for two minutes and increase weekly for another two minutes. If you are consistent with your practise, over time you will build to meditate for twenty to thirty minutes daily.

Today we are blessed with so much support from a variety of meditation styles. Choose a teacher or program that resonates with you, and you can download my meditation at www.catrionajones.com/bloomgirl.

Steep yourself in a world of Zen for at least one hour first thing every morning, and it will change your life. A commitment to your morning rituals is the most valuable gift you can give yourself, and you can build on these practices daily.

Emotional Freedom Technique, EFT (Tapping)

I love the emotional freedom technique (EFT) to start the morning clearing process. Also known as the tapping process, EFT is based on Chinese acupuncture and modern psychology. One taps on specific meridian points of the body and clears any blocks in the energy system. It alters your brain, energy system, and body all at once, positively impacting your physical, emotional, and mental well-beings.

The practice varies from tapping to energise or lift your mood to tapping through a variety of emotions or traumatic memories. It can also help bring to the light any subconscious limiting beliefs that might be blocking your goal achievement. As with all of these well-being tools and techniques, it is vital that we take full responsibility for our own well-being and seek professional experts for support if necessary.

It can feel a bit strange when tapping as we begin with a set-up statement which can sound and feel negative. However, the whole point of the exercise is to clear this negative energy and any repeat thinking patterns. We snap them at the root causes, at the deep cellular level. Louise Hay often said if we are going to clean the house, we need to know where the dirt is.

Tapping three to five points on the meridian points is recommended, as shown on the following diagram, and completing about five cycles. You can simply repeat the same phrase or create a script. Here is one of my favourite scripts.

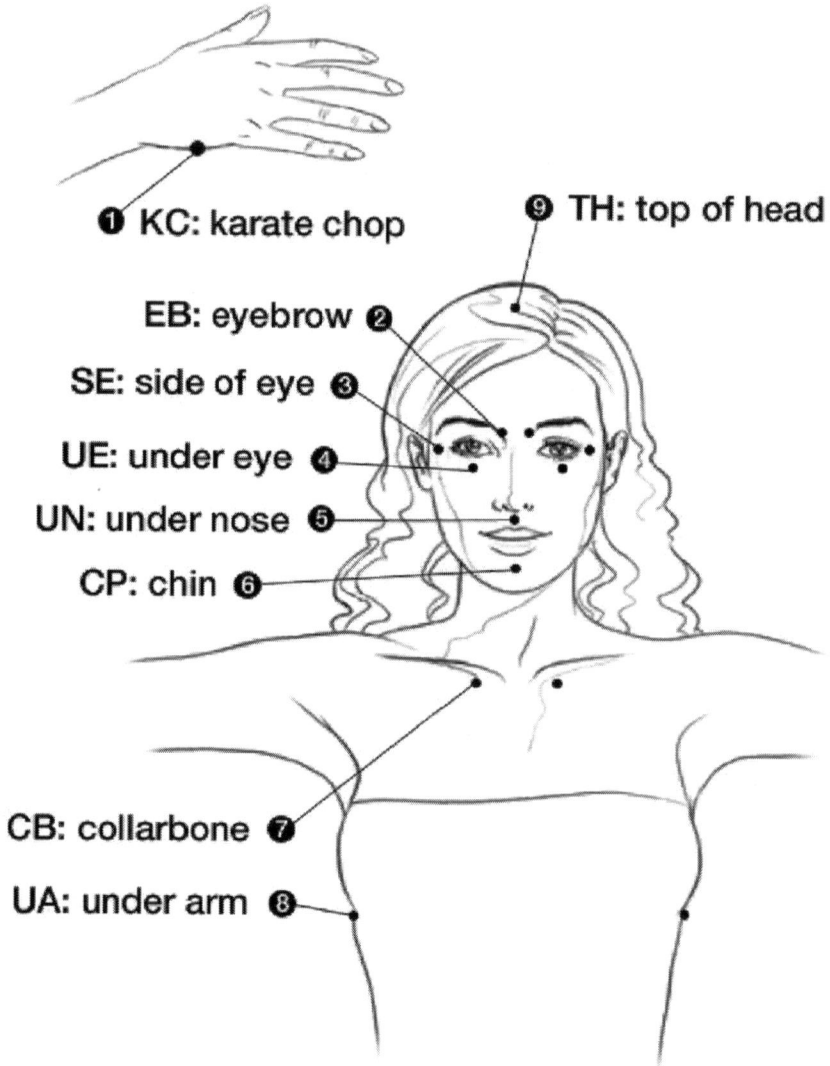

❶ KC: karate chop

❾ TH: top of head

EB: eyebrow ❷

SE: side of eye ❸

UE: under eye ❹

UN: under nose ❺

CP: chin ❻

CB: collarbone ❼

UA: under arm ❽

www.TheTappingSolution.com
(c) 2012 The Tapping Solution, LLC

Script: Relax, unwind, and catch some Zen.

Before I begin a tapping routine, I like to encourage my clients to take 3 deep breaths and measure their emotions on a scale of 1 to 10, for the benefit of the exercise, how stressed do you feel? We measure it on what I refer to as the Zenometer. You can download you own Zenometer to regulate your emotions and Zen levels throughout the day at www. catrionajones/bloomgirl.

On the scale, 10 is, 'I am completely stressed', and 1 is, 'I am completely relaxed and in my Zen.' Make a note of your score before you begin to measure your practice.

Round 1, with Set-Up Statement

Side of the hand:

> Even though I feel all this stress and overwhelm, I deeply and completely love, honour, and accept myself.
>
> Even though I feel drained and burnt out, I deeply and completely love, honour, and accept myself.
>
> Even though I feel so sensitive and exhausted, I deeply and completely love, honour. and accept myself.

Eyebrow: I feel overwhelmed and stressed.

Side of eye: I feel so drained.

Under eye: I am totally burnt out.

Under nose: It is all too much.

Under mouth (chin): Something has got to give.

Collarbone: Feelings of stress and being overwhelmed have become regular occurrences in my life.

Underarm: And I just can't seem to let it go.

Top of head: I want to learn to relax more in mind, body, and spirit.

Round 2

Eyebrow: All these feelings of being overwhelmed and stressed.

Side of eye: I feel disconnected from my body.

Under eye: It is all too much at times.

Under nose: And it is so uncomfortable.

Under mouth: Yet part of me knows.

Collarbone: I can figure this out.

Underarm: I have been taught to look outside myself for answers.

Top of head: Therefore, it makes sense I am out of my body.

Round 3

Eyebrow: It is time to figure this out once and for all.

Side of eye: I am curious about life without being overwhelmed and stressed.

Under eye: Oh, I often wonder what it would feel like to simply relax.

Under nose: Oh, I like the sound of relaxation.

Under mouth: Now it is time to relax.

Collarbone: All I have to do is be right here, right now.

Underarm: It is safe to relax.

Top of head: I can breathe gently and just let it all go.

Round 4

Eyebrow: Now it is time to come back into my body.

Side of eye: I am fully present in my body.

Under eye: I feel myself beginning to relax.

Under nose: I have been holding on to this tension for far too long.

Under mouth: It doesn't get me anywhere.

Collarbone: It is time to change my strategy and simply relax.

Underarm: I allow the stress to just melt away, and it is safe for me to just be.

Top of head: I am relaxed and in this moment.

Round 5

Eyebrow: I am okay.

Side of eye: I am at peace.

Under eye: I am calm.

Under nose: I am grounded.

Under mouth: I am centred.

Collarbone: I am a magnificent child of the universe.

Underarm: From this place of inner Zen, I am sure to fully bloom and show up as the best version of myself.

Top of head: It is safe for me to relax, connect with my inner Zen, and enjoy calmness in my mind, body, and spirit.

This is my time.

End of Tapping Routine

Take a deep clearing breath at the end of the exercise. Measure how you are feeling on the 1 to 10 scale, where 10 is totally stressed, and 1 is completely relaxed and in your Zen. You can repeat rounds, and as you feel the shift, you can simply repeat round 5 to seal and enhance the experience of a positive energy shift.

Some of the phrases I use personally and with clients or groups are simple. As an alternative to the ones listed previously is to use a phrase that describes exactly how you are feeling. For example, 'All this back pain', 'All this stress', 'All this anxiety', 'I am overweight' 'I cannot sleep.' You can simply follow the round and practice as guided above, repeat the same phrases with the relevant script you created. This is a very forgiving process, and you cannot get it wrong. Just keep tapping through the process until you feel a shift in your energy. Clients often notice a shift in their energy and feel lighter. Some can get emotional, yawn, or giggle. You might even become aware of more tension you have been holding on to. Don't judge it. Just look out for a shift.

I highly recommend the work of Brad Yates. Brad has supported me personally through the tapping process, helping me shift and grow, creating a breakthrough and quantum leaps. He runs great online classes and workshops. Brad is professional and supportive, and he embeds great humour into the process. You can access Brad's thousands of supportive tapping videos online. *The Tapping Solution*, with Nick Ortner and Jessica Ortner, is my other go-to. They run a very successful annual summit and have written great books on the subject. Their energy is loving, uplifting, and authentic.

Tapping is a great way to energise and set the body up for a deeper meditation practice. You can tap whilst absolutely anywhere. It is now common to see people tapping at their desks at work or on a train or even at the airport. It is simple and painless, and you can apply it to yourself. My clients have also found the tapping technique beneficial for anxiety, weight management, money blocks, physical pain, and sleep problems. It has helped people overcome insomnia and PTSD.

The Attitude of Gratitude

I once heard it said that a grateful heart cannot be angry. I love this saying. Although anger is a healthy emotion and a signal that something is out of alignment, there comes a time when we just want to let go and move on, or switch up the mood. There is also a time to feel and express our anger in a safe manner.

The practise of gratitude drops you right back down into the heart and shifts the energy. It can help us to make that shift we want from a low mood to a more uplifting mood. I begin every day with gratitude. I consciously decide to embed this practise into my morning rituals.

Some people like to begin their mornings by simply stating in their minds, '*Thank you for*', and list ten things that they are grateful for. I love to write this down like so: 'I am so happy and grateful that …' I find expressing my gratitude in written form puts more energy, feeling, and emotion into the practise of this exercise, really fusing me with the feelings and emotions, creating a positive and uplifting vibe.

We choose our thoughts, so we can decide to refuse to think negative thoughts first thing in the morning. The one ability and freedom that all human beings have is the ability to choose what they think; no person has the power to make that choice for us. The moment we make this decision and apply it to the beginning of our days, we own the day, and we will have a better day.

Whatever format or style you choose to carry out your daily morning gratitude, make your first thought a positive one to embed into your subconscious mind. The power is in choosing that first thought because we can wake up with some ugly thoughts. Gratitude will encourage your mind to wander and become creative and connected to everything in your life that you are truly grateful for, bringing you into harmony with source. You can write more than ten and keep going. As you practise all these exercises you will build that muscle and get better and better every day. The gratitude will flow naturally throughout the day too. Take a moment to reflect on what your first thoughts are in the morning and what new affirmations can you use to replace those negative thoughts that no longer serve you.

The Power of Affirmations

I would like to offer a word here on affirmations. When clients first begin to work with me, they often ask if I believe that affirmations work? I understand something that simple can almost appear a bit fluffy and fuzzy and maybe even twee. Affirmations are simply statements we say to make something firm, to declare what you do want, and to affirm as though something has already happened said in the present tense. Negative affirmations only confirm and attract more of what you don't want. We are not denying the challenges of the present but simply focusing on the hope of the future. Allow your affirmations to permeate your consciousness until they manifest for real. Your belief in affirmations is a key component to this journey in changing your power. It is vital to the process.

The most powerful way to say your affirmations is to look in your eyes while looking in a mirror. Positive vibes and thoughts will flow from affirmations work. But we must consciously choose the thoughts to develop and master a more positive mindset.

Saying affirmations is a very powerful tool when applied and used consistently. Wallace Wattle, in his book *The Science of Getting Rich*, said,

> There is a thinking stuff from which all things are made, which, in its original state, permeates, penetrates, and fills the interspaces of the universe. A thought, in this substance, produces the thing that is imaged by the thought. Man can form things in his thought, and by impressing his thought upon formless substance, can cause the thing he thinks about to be created.

Affirmations are the perfect precursors to our thoughts as it all begins in the mind. I like to journal daily my positive affirmations that reflect my current goals, continuously impressing my new life, the life I am truly deserving of, upon my subconscious, thereby reprogramming old tribal subconscious beliefs that no longer serve my higher self and divine master plan. Here is how I view my subconscious. My old programming was impressed upon my inner child, and I impress my new story upon her too. My inner child loves to be called Nina; a name given to me by my younger sister Leeann because she simply could not pronounce Catriona. I love it, and her daughters call me Aunty Nina, and I adore that too. Anytime I am affirming for a goal and reprograming a belief, I tell Nina, my Child Magical archetype, all the good news as though it has already happened. She has the potential for sacred beauty in all things and the belief that everything is possible! She receives it with delight and does not question or challenge my enthusiasm. Rather, she gets really excited with me and for me (in truth, us). This conversation is light and fun. I do not burden her with the how, of course. Our dialogue goes something like this with my vision board as a focal point.

Catriona: I am so happy and grateful now this is our newly built house by the ocean.

Nina: Oh, I love the sea. I love to swim.

Catriona: This is my perfect workspace, and I have the perfect team.

Nina: Oh, we can put flowers and bunting and buy new cushions.

Catriona: This is the stable yard for the horses.

And so on; I think you get the role play.

Nina always approves of my creativity and opulent lifestyle, and she is a great cheerleader. She really helps me emotionally connect with and become enthused with my goal. She makes me feel as if it has already happened. Nina inspires my creativity and spontaneity and puts a spring in my step, motivating me every day. 'More' is a word that comes easily to us, and we no longer subscribe to being humble; 'Self-praise is no praise', or, 'Who does she think she is?' do not serve our sovereignty in the world of raising everyone up.

I then hand the manifestation of this work over to my goddess within and warrior archetype, that know how to manifest with lightning speed.

Remember, as we persist with our affirmation work, any resistance will appear for clearing. We can expect this battle as a part of the clearing-out process of old stuff. Acknowledge the resistance, and embrace the critical voice in this process. If we ignore this stage of processing and healing of the pain body, we will create more struggle or even suffering. It is safe to feel, express, and release.

As we embark on our healing journeys, turning around the story, we parent and teach our inner children. We pick up the pieces on the story map and reprogramme our belief systems. This is the journey within to create a more beautiful life. Sometimes family systems create labels for siblings—the funny one, the clever one, the helpful one, the stupid one and so on. We may have felt unlovable and not good enough and seek the approval of others to validate ourselves in the world. If we are obsessing about what other people think about us, we are totally detached from our own essences and can morph into their versions of who we should be in the world. We learn to take care of ourselves, to nurture and cherish our vulnerabilities. And as Melody Beattie claims, detach with love and become co-dependent no more.

We pick up our own lives and stuff, set new healthy boundaries, and take care of our own feelings. Detaching from loved ones does not mean we do not care. It gives us space to love ourselves and pour from cups that are full, not empty. We can let go of chaos and drama, pivot or sidestep it, and step into calm and order. In doing so we attract others to do likewise. This is the most loving, miraculous action we can take for ourselves and loved ones.

The truth is we can create space to be all the things mentioned above— the funny one, the smart one, the bold and daring one, the beautiful one, the adventurer—and do not need to limit it to one role, one talent, or to put ourselves in specific boxes. Inner child healing embraces the celebration of your talents and creativity, and reconnects you to all the pieces you think or chose to believe you are not. This self-image work embeds new positive beliefs, putting you on a higher frequency and in alignment and harmony with your passion, desires, and divine purpose here on earth.

Your purpose = whatever pain you have overcome
+ your desires + your passions.

As I have mentioned previously, I held some distorted messages about myself and had very negative beliefs concerning my image. My wounded inner child was something I had to work very consistently on. Mirror work was one of Louise Hay's signature tools, and I struggled to look in the mirror and authentically compliment myself. I didn't want to as I held limiting beliefs around my self-image. But desperate to change and feel better, I gave it a go. Each day it got easier. I simply began by saying, 'I am willing to love myself', progressing to 'I love you', and then, 'I really, really love you.' A few weeks into this exercise I studied myself in the mirror, and I noticed my cheekbone sticking out. Confused and wondering if one of the children's elbows hit me or if one kicked me during the night (still toddlers and bed-hopping), I asked my husband to come and have a look. I showed him my sticky out cheekbone! He gently wisped the hair back on the other side of my face and said, 'It sticks out here too. It's your cheekbones.'

I sat down on the edge of the bed and realised that I was beginning to see my face for the first time. 'Catriona', I whispered gently and naturally, 'without doubt you are beautiful.' I was learning not only to like what I saw in the mirror but to love me. It felt so good. And it just kept getting better and then better as I healed my wounded inner child. As I opened up and radiated self-approval, people frequently complimented me, and our home felt full of love and joy.

My relationships improved, and I became less judgemental of others as I saw in them what I was beginning to see in me. As I became less judgemental of others, I experienced more inner peace and acceptance. From this newly found territory and journey within, life got easier and so much better. The affirmation work brought my negative beliefs to the surface, and I persisted with the positive statements and broke through to the truth: We are all beautiful, including me.

In this healing process of rediscovering the powerful you, I urge you to get support. Trust the process, and leave no stone unturned. Secrets and pain will only keep one stuck and sick. Love your inner child and hug the teenager within you; she may be the one who needs your attention the most. I believe that our limiting beliefs and insecurities are particularly heightened at this stage of life.

Later in my journey I learned to use the mirror work and positive affirmations when healing and reassuring any part of me, including my inner teenager. Witnessing our daughter navigate her way through this choppy stage of life brought my awareness to any unhealed pieces in my story or wounded places within. It can be distressing to observe young girls and women struggling to find their places in the world and navigate the bombardment of social media and celebrity lifestyles.

Healing your inner teenager is a very delicate piece but worth considering and wholeheartedly embarking on. Our teenagers are generally rebellious, and when acquainted with trauma in the past, this can rise to the surface at this stage of life. All teenagers need to be heard, seen, and approved of in the world.

I want to highlight that we do not need to go digging for broken pieces; these pieces will come to the light naturally in divine timing when a self-help programme is applied consistently and you are ready. When the student is ready, the teacher will appear, the exact teacher to support that particular piece of the puzzle. People will come and go in our lives, as often said, for a reason, season, or a lifetime. I am totally grateful for every lesson learnt whether in pain or pleasure. No matter how deep the issue and no matter how long you have carried it for, the possibility exists for you to set yourself free from this hurt and pain. You deserve to feel free, whole, and complete. You are free, whole, and complete.

Building inner confidence and resilience is critical, and we can do this simultaneously with our inner teenager, daughters, students, or any young women we are responsible for in life. In fact, I believe all women have a responsibility to be role models for the next generation and forage the path for them. Soothing affirmations, mirror work, reflective journaling are great tools for building self-esteem and giving young girls permission to be themselves. That's the role they will play out exceptionally well. As F. Douglas says, 'It is easier to build strong children than to repair broken adults.'

Our girls and daughters need to know that to be born a girl is a beautiful, divine gift of power and creativity for the world. I believe all girls need certain things to empower them so they bloom into healthy strong women. All babies need - to be held and loved when they arrive into the world, a healthy attachment with their caregiver, and bestowed with pure, unconditional love from conception. Babies need a secure start in the world and a consistent and safe harbour for soothing and nurturing. As they grow, girls need freedom to be spontaneous, creative, and actually have a childhood. When girls feel loved and secure, they will remain connected to their purposes and follow their stardom, organically sprouting from seedlings to open, blossom, bloom, and flourish.

In order to grow up strong and free, girls need a circle and sisterhood of empowering women around them. Role models and cheerleaders to hold space and encourage them as they develop and move towards womanhood, teaching them to respect the preciousness of their bodies and understand the joy and pleasure of intimacy. Building strong roots to grow and flourish as their true authentic selves. It is important to teach our girls to have multiple friendship groups and to step away from unwanted behaviours. They need to learn to value and respect themselves and their worth. Fair-weather friends do not contribute to the environment required to bloom and flourish. Consistency and positive vibes are the cornerstones for growth. As parents we have to step in and make tough decisions for our girls. We are not their buddies. Sometimes saying no as a parent is the most loving word we can give to our children.

As mothers and women, it is vital to be in our bodies, connected, and authentic. This will empower our daughters and girls who follow to be strong and resilient in the world. Owning our vulnerability and openly embracing our intuition as an intellect creates healthy and competent women of the future.

Women of the world, this is our time to take our places at the table as women in our authentic power. We no longer have to try to strive to be a man in male-dominated industries or emulate patriarchy to take our spots at the top. A woman connected to her feminine power will not allow any other voice to be stronger than her own.

The process to womanhood can be a beautiful, natural process. It doesn't need to be hurried but age appropriate. Let us create a movement where girls and women are constantly leaning in and supporting each other. Let us eradicate this mean girl culture that is often witnessed and played out in social groups, hurting, excluding, and bullying girls and women.

As mothers, it is natural to feel protective and angry if our daughters are being bullied or treated unfairly. Like a lioness, we leap to protect and attack, reacting to other people's insecurities and activating our own. Challenging, believe me I know. I don't always get it spot on, but I am more aware nowadays occasionally the heart races in, and logic and reasoning go out the window. Over the years I have learnt to develop more calmness and separate my triggers from our children's. As mammies, we have to do our inner work. Our children's experiences and perceptions are different from how we feel and experience the world. Chances are that if you are reading this book, you have already healed a lot of your past and cleaned up the emotional inheritance for them. Holding strong to our values and healing journeys will keep the job of parenting far less messy and distressing.

I appreciate what Steve Biddulph says about friendship skills in his book *10 Things Girls Need Most: To Grow Up Strong and Free:*

> There is a bigger reason why things have become so mean and nasty in girl-land. It's about the values around us. If life is all a competition—to be the prettiest, hottest, most popular, or the smartest in tests, or most athletic, then it's a miserable world for our daughters. There is no chance to be who you are and relax and find your own unique path. And competitors can never really be friends.

Let's say no to mean girl culture and create a movement where women simply raise each other up. Connect our girls to the fires in their bellies and align them with their true purposes, rekindling that passion over and over again.

Mirror Work

Like I said, mirror work was my success tool for improving my relationship with myself and living a more contented life. The mirror will reflect how you feel deep inside about yourself. It raises awareness around self-image and self-belief, and where in your life you might be resisting growth, achievement, and breaking through a pattern, shifting your paradigms.

I find mirror work most effective when I look into the mirror, into my own eyes, and speak the affirmations aloud as outlined. This self-talk can be a gradual process and is a powerful way to feed the subconscious and create new ways of thinking and being. Mirror work with positive affirmations transformed my self-beliefs and self-worth, and I continue to use them every day. You might feel a little uncomfortable or awkward to begin with, but these affirmations can help you progress on your mirror-work journey. You can even use humour to get you going. Blow yourself a kiss in the mirror, for example.

Here is a variety of affirmations I have shared in workshops and with clients depending on their willingness to do mirror work. If you skip mirror work in your toolkit, you are missing a great transformational tool. Give it ago. Have fun, and laugh out loud! Giggles galore allowed, and laughing does not have to turn to crying. (Just in case you were told otherwise.)

Mirror Affirmations

I am willing to like you.

I am willing to learn to like you.

I am willing to learn to love you.

I am curious to know more about what it would be like to love you.

I love you.

(Insert your name), I really, really love you.

Journaling

Journaling is another way of expressing and releasing emotions so they do not wallow around in our bodies, creating discomfort or illness.

Journaling is great after mirror work to express the experience, feelings, and thoughts created during the mirror-work exercise. The use of a pen can be healing and the journal a safe, non-judgemental space to vent. Allow the pen to be your voice, to release the negative feelings and emotions onto the page and out of the mind and body. You can simply write or choose to journal to your higher power and trust the God of your understanding with your confusion, dilemmas, and contemplations.

Benefits of Journaling:

- Lifts your mood
- Helps you process emotions
- Enhances overall well-being
- Releases stress and anxiety
- Raises awareness
- Connects you with you

The Power Life Script by Peggy McColl

The Power Life Script is a technique created by Peggy Mc Coll. This exercise really accelerated my growth and manifestations. I have always recited my affirmations, and it never dawned on me to record them! Thanks to Peggy's program, I regularly record my affirmations into my audio memo app on my phone and listen to them at least twice a day. This embeds my new life into my subconscious, reprogramming and conditioning the mind. I highly recommend this tool; you can download it www.peggymccoll.com/powerlifescript.

I find as I listen to my own voice reciting my dream life, I relax and automatically feel the outcome of my wishes fulfilled. I am hereby choosing the right thoughts, activating my invisible power to create positive feelings, and feeling my way to the results I desire and to success. Today I strive to always think from the future and end results. It is a quick and simple technique to activate your power every day.

An Overview of My Morning Rituals

6:00—Wake up and take supplements

6:05—Clearing prayer

6:10—EFT

6:20—Meditate

6:50—Journal gratitude and mirror work

7:05—Power life script

7:15—Reading/study

You can download your Morning Rituals Planner and customise your own schedule with templates and tutorials at www.catrionajones.com.

Divine Connection and Guidance

The morning rituals encourage waking up every morning feeling blessed and grateful for a wonderful life. We make the choice to be happy, in the moment, and to stay in the heart. The body becomes still, and the mind quietens more and more. As we reach a state of blissfulness, Zen connects us to our spiritual essences, and the veil between the physical and spiritual worlds becomes thinner. Great wisdom comes from this stillness. We can be still and just listen, activating the divine intelligence within, one that is abundant in creativity. This stillness can direct our words and actions. This is the power within that all the great sages, gurus, and teachers talked about. No more is needed than silence and stillness to move us beyond the thinking mind to strengthen the intellect of perception and will, intuition and imagination. This is indeed the direct route to the fertile soil of greater awareness and unending potential for abundance in life. The power really is in the present moment, and you can maximise your potential by offering up the first hour of your day to these well-proven morning rituals that will guarantee your success. Christ said, 'the kingdom of heaven is within' (Luke 17:21 New Testament Bible).

You are the awareness, the consciousness; the creator and you are not separate. This power and intelligence that is greater than you is in all of us. Mastery of life is letting go and becoming one with this greater consciousness. It then moves and speaks through us and does the work. The great tapestry of your beautiful life unfolds effortlessly.

What Is Your Sign from the Divine?

We often like to get creative about this connection. Clients ask me, 'But how do you know and trust this connection or message from God?' My response is because you feel it! It doesn't come from outside you. And for me, the energy is never in my mind. It is usually a warm, light sensation experienced anywhere from the top of my head down to the gut. It feels easy and gentle, safe and trusting. It can be a tingling sensation in the crown of my head or a feeling of warm expansion in my heart; it varies. There is no right or wrong, but it is important that you connect with this inner knowing and connection. Learn to navigate, set, read, and know your inner compass. I often have symbols like hearts or gold stars. I have clients who see angels, white feathers, red roses, starfish, or mermaids. Clients often talk about a loud, clear word arising in their consciousnesses, imprinting in their hearts. Nature often sends us signs, or we can receive them every day through other people. You can decide; you will know. Ask your higher power to show you a sure sign and trust that divine connection; trust the power of your heartfelt intention.

There are four main ways that you can transcribe and translate messages from Spirit or a higher consciousness.

1. Clairaudience—You hear.
2. Clairsentience—You feel.
3. Claircognizance—You know.
4. Clairvoyance—You see.

When we deepen our connections and faith in the divine, we relax and trust. It doesn't really matter what your connection with consciousness is as long as you connect. Many people enjoy the synchronicity of numbers as well as symbols in receiving messages from the divine. Talk to your higher power and angels. Open up that loving conversation and daily dialogue. My divine guidance has shifted over the years from a rigid religious system to a more free-flowing art of allowing spiritual belief. I still maintain a strong faith in Christ and Our Lady. I feel lovingly protected and guided by their light every day. The line and connection is clear, crisp, and pure. This place of knowing wisely reminds me of the eternal nature of myself and others.

Over the years I have experienced many blessings and now count my blessings daily. However, I have a significant date that became special before I realised or remembered the calendar significance in the Roman Catholic Church. The 8 December would often be a happy occasion with a marked celebration. It was the date that Geraint, my husband, proposed to me and the date I received my MA in education. Both so very precious memories as I learnt to trust and enjoy the harmony of a loving relationship without sabotage and was awarded a significant milestone in teaching, my purpose. A loving relationship and connection to my purpose have been two very critical cornerstones in receiving abundance in my life. Never doubt the power of light. Be realistic, my lovely, and believe in miracles daily. The significance of the 8th December is the Solemnity of the Immaculate Conception, for me a celebration of the divine feminine power. Our Lady of Knock, Queen of Ireland, is a soothing and nurturing energy in my prayer life.

> Golden Rose, Queen of Ireland, all my cares and troubles cease
>
> As I kneel with love before you. Lady of Knock, My Queen of Peace
>
> (Our Lady of Knock Hymn)

The Use of Pendulums

A pendulum is another tool that is used to connect with your higher source. You ask yes-or-no questions to help make decisions, clarify, and guide. The pendulum can be a small object attached to the end of a piece of string or can be bought in a crystal form. I find consulting my pendulum can be a very soothing and reassuring experience when I am quiet and still. I wouldn't use it for everything or massive decision-making in life, but I feel it can support my connection to higher consciousness.

In order to connect with your pendulum, these steps are helpful.

1. Cleanse your pendulum using sage, moonlight, or water.
2. Sit comfortably and press pause so you feel relaxed.
3. Hold the pendulum in your dominant hand, between the thumb and index finger.
4. Ask simple questions to find your yes and no answer. You can simply state, 'Show me yes, and show me no.' I like to state a few facts. For example: 'My name is Catriona', 'Today is Monday', 'I live in … ' The pendulum will connect to your energy and swing either circular clockwise, circular anticlockwise, vertical, or horizontal. You will find your yes, no, or sometimes a neutral.
5. Ask your questions around a topic to gain insight and guidance, and remain open.

We are all blessed with the intellect of intuition and we are all psychic. We can hear the whisper of Spirit when we are really quiet. I feel the unconditional love of my dear aunty Pauline every day, her love for beauty, and her humour. And I have connected with the support and encouragement of Louise Hay and Wayne Dyer during my writing. Louise's message is usually simple, one line such as, 'Trust the process; you are loved.' Wayne enjoys settling in for a chat. He makes me giggle, and I find his voice so soothing, 'You've got this', he tells me and reminds me of the way of the Tao as he understands my determination with work and achievement, impatience driving me to push against the current at times. My competitive nature is eager to jump to first place on the podium. He simply reminds me to take it to the creative and just be. It will unfold and be done.

> The master keeps her mind always at one with the Tao;
> that is what gives her her radiance. (Tao Te Ching 21)

Whilst connected to Spirit, my shoulders relax, and certainty appears as if by magic. The energy is soothing and reassuring, validating my work and gifts.

A Note on Sleep

It is vital that you have a Zen bedroom and a restful sacred space to put your head down to sleep at night. Ensure your bedroom is decluttered and minimalistic. Avoid electronics in the room. Choose soft lighting and soothing colour schemes, and use the same Zen suggestions here as for your Zen space. Sleep occupies one third of our daily routine, therefore, it is of significant importance that we consider it, especially as more and more of my clients have sleep problems. The mood we experience before sleep will affect the overall sleep experience we have. Choose happy thoughts, uplifting literature, and try not to go to bed angry. Be mindful of all your thoughts pre sleep and remember to connect with your future successful self, feeling as if everything is exactly the way you desire it to be. Neville Goddard offers this on the subject:

> Your mood prior to sleep defines your state of consciousness as you enter into the presence of your everlasting lover, the subconscious. She sees you exactly as you see yourself to be.

Zen Eating Habits

The art of eating and enjoying a meal, no matter how big or small, has become increasingly challenging due to a busy and sometimes chaotic world. Cultivating Zen whilst eating will create more pleasurable eating and healthy digestion, potentially eating less. It will help raise awareness and connection to our bodies and possibly reduce food cravings and problematic eating. I have found myself at times eating a half of a packet of biscuits when feeling stressed, with no memory of actually opening the pack or tasting the biscuits. Now I try to notice mindfully the movement of my hands as I reach to open the cupboard, neatly arrange the biscuits on a favourite plate, and mindfully taste and enjoy each biscuit. I let go of the judgement of quantity and be with my eating, tasting and enjoying. When I adapt this more Zen approach with food, I always eat less and enjoy exactly what I have eaten. Try to eat fresh, wholesome food and have colour on your plate!

Zen Eating Tips

1. Pause before you eat, and express gratitude for your meal.
2. Prepare the space and food elegantly.
3. Avoid distractions; chew and eat your food slowly.
4. Connect with taste, texture, and the smell of your food or drink.
5. Stop eating when you feel full, and gently store the remaining food for later.

Zen and Movement

Physical movement of the body boosts the flow of energy and raises awareness of connection to your physical body, forming an intimate relationship with the wisdom of your body. I have talked a lot about the body and how important and miraculous a vessel it really is. It works consistently every day, supporting our physical, emotional, mental, and spiritual well-being. The body loves to move, and if we listen carefully to how it responds to certain movements and exercises, we will intuitively know exactly what our bodies need and enjoy.

Movement and exercise are personal choices, and anything from a gentle walk, swim, run, or yoga class will have an overall positive impact on your body. Our choice of exercise may vary in accordance to our monthly cycle, and we can sometimes resist movement. This is critical and can change by the time we as women arrive at perimenopause and prepare to access the full depth of our womanly wisdom. I know that I always feel so much better after as little as a twenty-minute walk or yoga workout. Swimming can leave me feeling even more exhilarated and reinvigorated when I get out of my head and the story about the getting changed process and into the water! Water has the amazing power to connect us with the space of our origin, the womb, enhancing our feminine intuitions and psychic abilities, especially if you can get into the sea.

Benefits of Movement on Your Overall Well-Being

Physical benefits
- Reduces weight
- Strengthens muscles and bones
- Increases blood and oxygen flow

Emotional benefits
- Boosts mood
- Reduces anxiety
- Improves sleep

Mental benefits
- Strengthens healthy brain structure as neurons connect
- Sharpens focus
- Supports mental health and growth mindset

Spiritual benefits
- Nurtures the vessel of your energy system
- Helps unblock chakras

Zen Movement Breaks

Zen movement breaks are highly recommended throughout the day, particularly if you work at a desk. It is a good idea to become aware of how long your body likes to sit at any one time. It can vary from twenty minutes to sixty minutes, depending on the individual. It is important you know what your body likes and honour your needs. You will be more productive, focussed, and energised with occasional two- to five-minute breaks, stretching, walking to the water machine (avoid distractions), a tapping routine, or perhaps getting some fresh air.

There is plenty of research to support the benefits of movement breaks, and when I studied for my MA in education, I conducted some of my own action research, embedding Accelerated Learning Techniques by Alistair Smith into the classroom with the children. He illustrates how effective, balanced, and brain-based learning is rich, multi- path, and multi-sensory, and promoting movement and variety in activities can stimulate the brain in a positive way, preventing stress and feelings of being overwhelmed. This 'braingym' had a positive and significant impact on the overall behaviours, moods, and achievements of the students.

Benefits of Zen Movement Breaks

- Improved concentration
- Increased productivity and quality of work
- Reduced stress
- Increased work satisfaction
- Boosts team morale

Bloom Girl Exercise 7

1. Create a sacred zen space.
2. Press pause.

Remember to customise your morning rituals to suit you!

Summary

There are many suggestions here, and the Zen toolkit is one that can be developed and deepened over a lifetime. It is recommended that you choose one or two techniques to start with. You really want to create a win-win situation with your Zen routines. And remember not to try too much too soon. This is a gentle process, not linear or academic lessons. I recommend you introduce the pause twice a day, and practise gratitude to get you started. Keep your routine simple, and start with those two things. You can embed a new tool weekly and gradually build your practise to ensure growth and consistency. And you, my lovely, are guaranteed to blossom and bloom.

You can download the morning rituals planner and join the group for more support at www.catrionajones.com.

CHAPTER 5

Goal Achievement

Let the egg meet the sperm and create a miracle,
something divine and beautiful.

The egg, the feminine energy, is present in her being, knowing, and openness to receiving. Therefore, it is time to connect with the masculine energy and take inspired action. Now that you have set your inner compass in the direction of your dream life, it is time to lock in your goals. The process of goal achievement is one of simultaneously and continuously clearing any emotional blockages that are getting in the way of pressing on and holding steadfast to your vision and results. It is now time to switch it up to some technical tools for mapping out, measuring, and successfully achieving your goals.

A useful piece in the goal achievement process for women is understanding masculine and the feminine energies. In describing both energies this is not a reference to male and female; they move beyond gender. They are simply the two energies required for the law of gestation and creation. However, there is usually more feminine energy in a woman and more masculine energy in a man, but this is continuously evolving. Feminine and masculine energies do not have to be perfectly balanced, as in 50-50, but both need to be present for the success of your goals, particularly the feminine ability to receive and the masculine ability to create and follow systems and structures. Success is measured by how efficiently we co-create using the universal laws. The seven laws of the universe that I have referred to in this book illustrate and demonstrate how one can do less and accomplish more. I will share with you my understanding of the feminine and masculine energies.

Feminine energy is referred to as yin and includes intuition, imagination, nurturance, gentleness, creativity, and power. It is usually thought of as water soft and flowing. The yin energy expresses her emotions, is unafraid to feel, receives, and let's go when required. She lives in accordance with the natural rhythm and circular cycles of life such as the moon. The feminine energy needs expression and creation. In my coaching I often refer to this energy as 'The Goddess Within'.

Masculine energy, yang, is more thrusting, structured, and linear. The masculine energy of the sperm races toward the egg, and we only need one out of millions. One inspired action to create, produce, and birth new life. Masculine energy is direct and one of strength, willpower, focus, and clarity. He is both the protector and the planner. He is linear and usually follows a plan. Masculine energy is like granite. In my coaching I refer to this energy as 'The Warrior Within'. Granite may be strong and grounded, but water will eventually shape shift anything it comes in contact with.

The Feminine Energy—Yin	The Masculine Energy—Yang
Moon	Sun
Passive	Direct
Soft	Hard
Being	Controlling
Circular	Linear
Intuitive	Logical
Creative	Decisive
Imagination	Focus
Nurturing	Protective
Expressive	Structured
Random	Intellectual
Flowing	Rigid
Receiving	Giving
Experiencing	Achieving
Patient	Urgent
Subconscious	Conscious

If we look to nature and how the divine is expressed and animated through us in the process of human birthing, we can get a clearer understanding of the feminine and masculine working together. Let's take conception for example. The egg just waits and embraces the art of allowing. She gets on the frequency of her desires and waits to magnetically attract it. It is drawn to her. She trusts divine intelligence and her magnetism and invisible power. The sperm is unafraid to take action and mechanically heads in a forward direction to its target.

When both are in balance, we feel most harmonious and fulfilled. This can be applied to any creation in life; trust and connection to your goal with inspired action to activate the process and birth, a journey from conception to creation with both energies. As women we can block our innate abilities to receive and sabotage success with distraction, acting on too many things as opposed to inspired action in the direction of a clear target.

My Story

In understanding the law of gestation, I can identify times when the imbalance of the energies have been present and operating within me throughout my life. Moved and excited by a new creative idea, I would act on almost everything as opposed to taking logical or inspired action. My journey, particularly as a female entrepreneur, was steeped in the feminine energy of imagination and creation but lacked clarity of direction, structure, and focus, and an inability to fully receive.

During my teaching career I became unfulfilled and uninspired in the didactic education system that I followed. Following a spiritual awakening, I experienced a great burst of desire and creativity. I became very excited about life. I intentionally use the word 'excited' as a lot of the ideas were coming from outside me. At this stage of my journey, I was unable to discern what I was admiring on the outside or enthused by from within. So, I acted on lots of things—if not everything—whilst steeped in an explosion of creativity. Not a good idea. Zen is required to be discerning and effectively bloom to flourish in the world.

I loved the freedom of being a female entrepreneur, and opening a gift boutique fed my burst of creativity. Although my business grew to win awards, I was definitely going round in circles. The struggle of retail and my lack of planning moved me through a number of services. I offered coaching, intuitive readings, furniture painting, motivational talks, and retail! This was an extensive gift range that expanded into ladies' accessories and clothes. I was overwhelmed and burnt out. It was a continuous struggle to make ends meet, and I had no idea what I was crafting from one month to the next. I was caught up in the paradigm of work struggle and hardship, creating, recreating, over giving, and not receiving.

I took a step back, engaged in a reflection process, and reconnected with what I loved and my purpose. It brought me immediately back to teaching and coaching, a deep yearning to inspire others to overcome. I took a leap of faith, closed the shop and focussed on mastering my craft, embracing the masculine energy to structure my business. I was blessed to have the experience of my husband simultaneously building his business. As I went with the circular flow of creativity, he stuck to one service, learnt to master his craft, and became the go-to for his services, building his business to its maximum capacity, effortlessly open to receiving the abundance of the universe. He conducted his business straightforwardly every day, communicating in a direct and assertive manner.

I offer a heartfelt note to fellow female entrepreneurs and women in business: You do not have to offer every service under the sun. Remember to stay connected with what you love, and allow time for gestation. In the past I often became distracted in my business, particularly at times when it was a struggle. It is vital that we embrace the masculine energy of will and focus. It can be challenging at times when you see other female entrepreneurs who appear to be succeeding and make it look easy. Believe me, making it look easy is the hard bit. You have no idea what their success story looks like, and there is usually a messy bit in the middle.

Avoid comparisons; it's the thief of joy. I know as women we can get into the competitive field with playground politics of 'my idea'. Know this for sure, my lovely. No person can ever steal from you what the divine has placed in your heart. Focus on what you really love. Get really good at it, and you will lead and own that field. It is your birth right. Take it from the competitive field to the creative always, and you are guaranteed to prosper. Set you inner compass needle to face joy, and purpose and freedom will be yours for keeps. Purposeful and free.

Wallace D. Wattles says,

> You must get rid of the thought of competition. You
> are to create, not to compete for what is already created.

Masculine energy helped me ground the feminine energy and get crystal clear about my services and brand. This effectively taught me to harness the practical skills of structures within my business, owning the cash flow system, record-keeping, having figures at my fingertips, and overall getting comfortable with the new title of businesswoman. If all the sperm were to break the wall of the egg, the mother would struggle to nurture and develop all her babies. As women we are now ready to move from the multitasking to focusing on one job at a time, master our crafts, and do them exceptionally well. I once heard the working in harmony with both energies compared to gardening. The masculine energy maps out the plan, structure, and boundaries. The feminine energy embeds the flow and creativity of shrubs, plants, colours, and features, nurturing and watering the plants to welcome and receive the harvest and bloom season.

We have already spent time exploring and exercising your invisible powers and creativity, strengthening your intellect of imagination and intuition. We have worked on how to ask and vibrate to attract. In this capsule I want to support your clarity and focus so that you can *will* your goals to you by applying all the masculine and feminine energy required. We align with nature's intelligence, and our dreams are fulfilled.

I like to use the ABC goal theory system as designed by Bob Proctor.

> Your Goals
>
> A-type goal—You know you can do it.
>
> B-type goal—You think you can do it.
>
> C-type goal—A stretch goal, but you have no idea of how to do it. It is so big it scares you but excites you at the same time.

For example:

> A-type goal—Buy a new car.
>
> B-type goal—Up your business level to a six-figure income.
>
> C-type goal—Create a movement that globally empowers you to create financial freedom in your life.

The majority of people set A-type goals. In order to achieve a C-type goal, we must grow into a C-type goal person. We have to apply all the tools and techniques outlined in this book. What are you prepared to do to get there? It is time to get to work on your big stretch goal, and you will start to develop your action mindset and develop and firm up success-oriented behaviours. You become the greater you in the process.

It is so much about the journey along the way. Stop blaming and stop complaining. Don't look left, don't look right, just do it! Make your schedule your new BFF, and create a loving, intimate relationship with time. As women we need to reprogram ourselves to know that there is enough time. When we actually hold ourselves accountable for the twenty-four hours in the day we realise this truth. That is why a schedule is critical to plan our days. I include all my activities and tasks in my schedule, such as school run, preparing dinner, family time, and study time. In owning my schedule, I get the jobs done. If you don't schedule, chances that it will happen are unlikely. If we are serious about and committed to stepping into our power as women and claiming our spaces in the world, we have to delegate. Very few women achieve a C-type goal alone. Ask yourself, 'Who else can support me with this?' Do you need help with collecting the kids a few days a week perhaps, a housekeeper, cleaner, or virtual assistant?

Your C goal has got to be a great big goal that makes you want to leap out of bed in the morning. And your why has got to come from the heart. My why makes me cry. Everything I strive to do is for the healing of my inner child and our children that they may always feel loved and supported in a nurturing environment of abundance in every form. Your C goal has to be bigger than your greatest hurt in life.

Get clear on what you desire. Write your goal in the centre of the goal sheet planner provided in the workbook, and create a mind map of action steps towards your goal.

Mind Mapping

Mind mapping helps you formulate a to-do list. In order for your goals to be achievable, they must be measurable. The stretch goal will impact all other goals and areas of your life. After putting all your ideas on paper so you can continue to develop along the way, it is time to commit to action. I find that ninety days is a good, measurable time frame to work within. It is a great way to check in, review, and evaluate. As we build momentum and make progress, we can take great strides, and ninety days give us the opportunity to challenge ourselves and step up the pace. Evaluate and reflect. If it is not working on any level, refine, pivot, and shift the strategy, always moving towards your target goal.

What Smaller Tasks Can You Start on Today as Part of Your C-Goal Process?

You might have a money goal. Write the money goal in the centre of your mind map. On the lines leading out from the centre, record all the income-producing activities or services that you can create (the services/work you love) and actions in order to manifest this money. What will you give in exchange for this service? In his book *Think and Grow Rich*, Napoleon Hill is very clear about asking for the exact amount of money and the services you intend to render in order to receive it.

Mind Map Example

Step 1. Name the goal in the centre of your mind map.

Step 2. List headings of the task categories

Step 3. Draw lines radiating outward from each line, with more details on action tasks. Break down each again.

The 90-Day Mind Map Goal Planner is available with the Bloom Girl workbook. Once you have worked the map down to the mini-action steps, you need to estimate how long it will take to complete these actions. Estimate your overall investment time needed for this area of your goal. If your goal takes longer than anticipated, keep going; it is an incredibly worthwhile process, and you are on your path. Daily action is critical to your success. It is vital that you now have income-producing action steps from this mind map embedded into your daily schedule. Actually write it down. Decide on how much daily action you will commit to and complete each week.

Get an Accountability Buddy

Share your commitment and goal with someone you trust, your partner or a friend, for example. An accountability buddy is very helpful. This might be someone you can share your weekly action steps with and be accountable to at the end of the day. I find a weekly meeting with an accountability buddy very supportive and useful to my productivity.

I also like to check in at the end of the day. This is often in the form of a tick message to illustrate complete. Make your goals and task measurable.

Having a schedule and mini-tasks in support of your goal ensure you are taking action, making progress and engaging in income-producing activities (IPA). The quality of your work and efforts will be in correlation to the quality of your daily habits. You need to see it and feel it in your mind's eye before you can experience it in reality. Manifesting and achieving will then come easily to you.

The law of assumption will also speed up the goal achievement process for you. Ask yourself this simple question: 'Now that my goal is achieved, how do I feel?' What would your future self be like as the achiever of the C goal. Think and behave like that powerful woman now. Act as if now. Remember, resistance will show up, particularly at the early stages of manifestation. The wounded child or orphaned child shadow behaviour is likely to be activated in this process. Awareness is again the key here. Learn to be very clear about what resistance looks like for you. It can be the wounded child running the show and show up as fear, feeling unwell, procrastination, avoidance, excuses, distraction. It is amazing—and soul-destroying—what chaos and drama we are possible of creating to take ourselves out of the game.

Here are some questions I ask myself daily to stay on track. They are worth exploring and help embed the law of assumption into my day.

My Future Self

What does she look like?

How does she dress?

How does she conduct herself?

How would she handle this situation?

111

How does she respond to distraction and low-level energy in her environment?

What would she be doing now with her time?

I also have a bank of key phrases when negative chatter or self-doubt creeps in, particularly at the end of the day, when the will begins to weaken.

What other people think of me is none of my business.

If not me, who? I am enough!

I am deserving and breaking through any resistance to ancestral healing.

There is more room at the top, girl.

If you are the smartest person in the room, you are in the wrong room unless you are being paid.

The comments and phrases in the previous exercise are not meant to be derogatory or belittling to others but to keep me on track and staying on the path of the opulent life I deserve. And they can do the same for you. I am holding only to the truth that I am deserving of a more beautiful life. Being true to me and raising my frequency will empower others to do so also. In the words of John F Kennedy 'A rising tide lifts all boats'.

The Goal Achiever

She is determined and has had enough of playing small. She honours the deep yearning within her to fully bloom. In understanding the laws of nature, she knows that this divine perfection is also deep within her. She connects emotionally to her dream and vision for her beautiful life; she sees it as already done. She is confident her dreams can be manifested. All thoughts and words lead to the core heart centre of her wishes fulfilled, and she knows that with a clear, detailed goal, the universe will meet her there. Her schedule is one of practical steps towards achieving her goal and taking inspired action. And finally, she receives with grace.

The achiever is destined to bloom and avoids distraction. She is no longer concerned about the paths of others unless to follow their greatness, support, lead, or inspire. She knows that what the divine has implanted in her heart is her sacred contract, and no one can steal or take it; it must manifest into form. In fulfilling her dream, she is constantly shifting her mastery to the creative and avoids the competition at all costs. Self-care and self-love have become her new ways of consciously living in the world. She is indeed a radiant goddess.

The achiever catches glimpses of herself in the mirror because she is her own competition. She strives to improve herself and do better every day, eyeballing herself square on she declares, 'I have got this.' She knows how to give herself a command and follow it. Her internal navigator is switched on to discipline. She has mastered her mindset and is heartfelt and connected to Spirit with faith. She became a conscious, living woman with high standards and a beautiful and open heart. She shifted from fear to love to personal feminine power.

She reclaimed her femininity, goddess power, and purpose from within and is hardwired once again to the feminine energy of her intellect, imagination, and intuition. This brings all her desires to her effortlessly. She is always blooming, and weeds have no chance of survival in her energy field. Her masculine balance of focus and will adheres to her command and serves her well. How could she or anyone have ever doubted her suitability to success? Feeling has become the secret to activating her superpower. She has fully reclaimed her feminine power to receive in the world and harnessed the masculine power of structure.

In conclusion, as you embark on your journey to flourish in life, trust in the process of life, my lovely. Today I only look over my shoulder to see how far I have come. I spent many years in competition with others and self-criticism of my not 'enoughness' belief, comparing my inside with their outsides. Flowers don't compete with each other; they simply bloom, and each is as beautiful as the next, an array of colours, patterns, shapes, textures, and expressions even within a bouquet of the same flowers. It is also okay to bloom alone for an episode of life. I would often beat myself up for being too sensitive, disown the empath within me, and become frustrated with my strong emotional connection. What we consider to be our defects are very often our superpowers, and as women, our feminine energy is our superpower. Set the intention to own your fertility, free-flowing and feeling nature fully. We can use this creativity, imagination, and intuition to step into our powers, fully open and bloom, manifesting a divine garden of wisdom and beauty one bud at a time—The bloomers. You take a stance and demand respect in all areas of your life.

We teach people how to treat us through our energies and boundaries. When we internally and energetically hold negative beliefs about ourselves, people can energetically and intuitively sense this and respond to the signals we send out from our energy fields. Nothing can mask this energy or vibration, so weed it out. Clean up your energy field. As we do the inner work and learn to love and approve of ourselves daily, we trust life and believe that life really wants the best for us, that the universe has our backs. The energy shifts, and people begin to reflect to us the self-respect we carry within. They experience the God within us, emulated and embodied through our authentic goddess energy.

Today I trust the process of life and appreciate that I am part of its natural flow and rhythm. I believe and have faith in a power that is greater than me but flows through me every day. I didn't always have this deep faith, and I spent many years seeking approval and pushing to have things my way. Pushing for people to see and understand my point of view was constantly uphill and exhausting, leaving me feeling depleted. I did not have the inner road map to understand how I felt and experienced life, and I was unable to navigate another route without the tools. Thankfully today I know better. In the past I endeavoured to be understood rather than to understand. Today I am guided by the prayer of St Francis of Assisi to see the other person fully. In seeing them I am seeing me and honouring the divine that is within every single human being on this earth,

Dear Lord,

Grant that I may seek rather to comfort than be comforted, to understand than to be understood, to love than be loved.

Everyone has her own journey and has her own story. We have no idea of the hurt that others carry. But we can be sure of one thing: They have been hurt too. That's the ebb and flow of life, the law of polarity.

Feeling into the past guides us to the wounds of the past to heal. From this point of acknowledgement and reflection, we can then shift perspective to view the world from a different lens. There has to come the time when you decide to stop dwelling on the past but only go there to share your story and move on. It is a quantum leap to realise and accept that you are no longer that little girl governed by those limiting and outdated tribal belief systems. There is another way, a better way perhaps, a different perspective. Always consider other possibilities, and stay open and neutral. Viewing the world from a healed wound is much lighter and free-flowing. A simple glance will remind us of how far we have come, and any attention the wound requires we can attend to with our customised toolkit of self-love.

A flower blooms in the right environment nurtured by the correct measure of light and water. There is research to prove that the energy of the environment also contributes to its growth and beauty. Keep good company, remain patient, and trust. We do not have to pull open the petals of the flower.

Feeling in the present reminds us of the stillness and safety in the world when staying centred and grounded. When we practise meditation daily, we are set up to practise mindfulness in our days. I personally can feel focussed for six to eight hours following my morning mediation practice, responding as opposed to reacting or over-reacting. We can operate from a place of calm as opposed to one of fear and anxiety, minimising the damage throughout the day and being able to relax in the evening with a happy heart. From this place of calm, we gain more clarity, focus, make good decisions, and boost creativity, therefore operating in flow and honouring the divine wisdom within ourselves.

Feeling into the future and connecting with our dreams will guarantee success. Feeling is good in the right measure. We journey within and embrace our perfectionism there. We dissolve any negative feelings or disbeliefs that are out of alignment when connecting to this essence, letting go of resentment, anger, fear, guilt, and shame. The journey within is the path to embracing natural beauty and authenticity and abandoning the story of 'I need to fix or improve my appearance.' Feeling into the future supports our dreams; we can imagine and connect with our future selves there.

Beauty and Aestheticism

The magical child within me is on a mission to encourage myself and others to see order and beauty as a way of life. It is so pleasing and soothing, and it brings me fully present with art and the divine. I guess the whole conversation resonates with me as it is close to my own encounter and personal struggle with the polarity of beautiful and ugly, and who or what title or label belongs where and with whom. I have always loved detail and creativity, and I guess it really is personal taste and, 'Beauty is in the eye of the beholder', when it comes to my choice of a dainty teacup, random-coloured lipstick, embroidered cushion, or elegant frock. It connects me deeply with my life of purpose and intention and lights me up.

Oscar Wilde said we spend our days looking for the secret of life when the secret of life is art. Oscar Wilde was one of Ireland's finest writers and known for his wit and flamboyance with an armful of lilies, lavender gloves, and feathered hat. He spoke regularly about beauty and aesthetics, and I agree that it is indeed a worthwhile art form that can dominate an approach to life encouraging appreciation of our environment and its ability to connect us with peace, pleasure, and joy within.

When we opt for peace and choose stillness, the inside job, life becomes more about being than doing. The world is currently caught up in a huge industry of cosmetic surgery and image adjustment procedures to boost mood and self-esteem. The image of ourselves that we hold in our hearts and minds can be very powerful. I am not completely dismissing the benefits of surgery; it can be life-changing for people. I do believe that we have to be cautious and realise that 'the doing path' is never ending. Where does the self-criticism, desire to improve, and plastic surgery end? You decide, and ensure that only you are the one holding the measuring stick for that. Power and control over your image are in your safe hands, and not the media, the celebrity world, the abusive partner, the judging mean girl, or work colleagues. Make an informed choice, a trusted service, authentically and empowering you to honour your needs and desires.

The journey within will guarantee stillness, peace and effortless success. The connection to our hearts will remind us that everything and everyone is beautiful in their natural states. The same fundamentals that apply in nature apply to us too. Pressing pause and meditating will bring us to that place of rest; the calm will permeate our entire essence. It will be present in our energies, the way we speak, our poise and manner, even in the natural radiant glow of our skin as we embody the irresistible fragrance of deep, authentic self-approval of ourselves and others.

I have experienced extreme restlessness and agitation in my life and took a good shot at seeking approval outside me. It was exhausting and just added more grief and disapproval. In the past I often used many methods to soothe my discontentment with self-image, including shopping binges, overeating sugary foods, and late-night clubbing. This only created an appetite of more, more, more and did not help me navigate towards the root cause of my low self-worth, no matter how hard or extreme I pushed. I stepped into my power when I had the ability to look in the mirror at my true reflection and courageously deconstruct the negative chatter and story, rebuilding a positive self-image from this point and a lasting transformation on solid foundations. There is something eternal about paying attention to this reflection and learning to love the girl in the mirror. When we arrive at this point of hearing and soothing, we arrive at the sweet spot of a positive self-image and radiate a glow that no cosmetic company can bottle. This antiaging beauty secret is within, the limitless and the master key to freedom to be the authentic you. You will find you do you best.

As mothers, grandmothers, aunts, big sisters, godmothers, guardians and teachers, we pass this wealth of inheritance on to our girls. Remember that in the words of Dr Christiane Northrup, 'You are a radiant ageless Goddess.'

One weekend my husband, children, and I were enjoying a morning walk around the lovely Rathmullan, Donegal. We parked our camper van at the seafront and took a walk along the shore and this small, quaint town. We were relaxed and happily enjoying the creativity embraced by the locals in the painting of their doors, decorated porches and courtyards of the houses and cottages. It was fun and heartfelt. As we rested on a wall at the end of our walk, two ladies approached wearing swim costumes and modestly wrapped in beach towels. My husband teased them on their bravery as they approached the sea as it was cloudy and cool. They giggled and admired his Welsh accent. 'I am happily retired now', said one lady, 'after forty years of working in Dublin. This is my sister, and we do this swim every morning.' The children were niggling us to come on and stop staring, but of course we had to enjoy the magic of watching them enter the sea. They efficiently put on their swim caps and goggles, smiled and waved at us, and then bobbed away like two wee ducks, two vibrant sisters, free and easy, in great spirits.

My heart was happily connected to their friendliness, joy, and fun, and I acknowledged there is something so reassuring and assertive in women who are sixty years and older. Most women at this age are completely comfortable in their own skins and exude inner contentment, almost completely eradicated from the plague of self-doubt. Walking away and heading back to the camper van, a little sadness lurked inside me as I wondered why it takes women all these years to connect with our wisdom within and that deeper knowing that we are good enough and have nothing to prove to the world. We are radiant goddesses. Let's embrace this knowing sooner in life, and impress that upon our daughters' enoughness for the world. What a daily dip in the ocean can do for the soul! Thank you for your goddess beauty and wisdom, lovely sisters of Rathmullan, and for sharing your giggles galore with the world. You see, sharing a compliment, a joke, and joy with one person has a ripple effect, just like the sea, and can be felt and experienced by so many. Choose to send a ripple of fun out into the world today. A smile or a hello can go a long way, and its imprint might even last forever in the heart. It may be the message of hope that another is needing at that time, a reminder that there is good and divine in all of us, so simple, pure, and contagious.

I honour the divine present in every human being on this earth. And I know for sure that when we grow and raise our consciousness, we influence each other and are all one. It may appear a little contradictory that with this in mind I write to an audience of women and girls. But through my own study of patriarchy and the guidance of Dr Cathy Higgins, I believe that if we were to dismantle patriarchy, we would get to the root cause of separation in humanity. It is also my wish that men may find my message helpful and supportive—fathers, grandfathers, teachers, godfathers, uncles, in fact all men.

In her book *The Stories We Tell: Reimagining Human Relations* (2019), Cathy Higgins uses feminist theologian Carol Christ's definition of patriarchy as a basis for understanding the roots of patriarchy in a culture of war and militarism, and its impact on women, dominated people, and the land and its resources in the context of Northern Ireland and the Republic of Ireland. Carol Christ defines patriarchy

> as a system of male dominance rooted in the ethos of
> war which legitimates violence, sanctified by religious

symbols, in which men dominate women through the control of female sexuality with intent of passing property to male heirs, and in which men who are heroes of war are told to kill men, and are permitted to rape women, to seize land and treasures, to exploit resources, and to own or otherwise dominate conquered people.[1]

Women and men are oppressed, in different ways, within a patriarchal society. It disempowers women in the world, and men are often stripped of their feminine energy to feel, express, and emotionally connect with the world.

A patriarchal society promotes male privileges and is male-centred, but it serves no one fully. I mean, is it any wonder women struggle with prosperity, their money story, feminine power, and repress their sexual desires? Patriarchy is not just about male dominance and female control. It refers to society and how we have all dealt with male privileges and the consequences. Evidenced by the disempowerment of women and the reality of being left powerless, to squabble amongst ourselves for any scraps of power left over from the scramble for power by men: patriarchy created a belief within us of scarcity and lack.

It is now our time to endeavour to support each other, encouraging and supporting, respecting women in leadership and positions of authority. I have witnessed how the shadows of patriarchy can play out in female-dominated work environments. A new male leader is appointed, and he arrives and claims his title as the boss. A new female leader arrives, begins to direct and instruct, and she's a bitch. She is often disliked and challenged. In her fear and isolation, she emulates patriarchy to manage the situation and gain respect. Thus, bullying in the workplace can become prevalent within and between genders.

We don't know what we don't know, and we have all contributed to this dynamic of society at some stage. I know for sure I certainly have

---

[1] Carol P. Christ, "A Definition of Patriarchy: Control of Women's Sexuality, Private Property and War," *Feminist Theological Journal* 24, no. 3 (2016): 214.

been bullied and exiled, and in my defence and fear, my reaction was to bully. We often turn to the shadow archetypes until we raise our awareness and consciousness in life. A Course in Miracles reminds us we choose between two minds, fear or love, and we often detour to fear but can always return to love.

Repeat after me, 'We are all in this together.' Our boys and men need support also to become positive, contributing members of community. Many of whom need freed from false power, from the demons of alcohol, drugs, gambling, gaming, and the long list of addictions society is battling with today, experienced by all genders. The social structures and absenteeism of the elders are no longer available at times to guide and initiate boys into maturity and manhood. In his book *Adam's Return: The Five Promises of Male Initiation*, Richard Rohr describes the need for the initiation of boys. He claims, 'Initiation is not about being a warrior as much as it is about being conscious, awake and alert'. The consequences of not honouring this sacred journey and process is a wounded community.

> But if your original wounding is not healed, every man you meet has to deal with the brokenness of your father, and every women you meet faces your mother's unresolved issues—which you inherited—not to speak of your own store of personal memories and hurts.

Richard Rohr suggests a truly spiritual and wise initiation for young boys must somehow address all four parts of a man's soul. We must affirm, educate and validate the following archetypes in a healthy and balanced way – The Warrior, The Magician, The Lover and The King.

As mothers we can learn to accept the beautiful nature of the male soul. Female power can be found in loving, open, authentic dialogue—I am talking woman to woman, mother to mother. An opportunity is indeed created for the feminine spirit to speak. I have a friend, Bridgín, and she is one of those uplifting women who emulates, personifies, and expresses the goddess and priestess wisdom effortlessly. I reached out to this recently to avail of her experience as a mother to several sons.

Well, you know she had walked the path, and I can happily admit I knew very little about teenage boys. She lovingly soothed my fear and anxieties and left me feeling strong and excited about the next stage of our parenting journey. I thanked her profusely as she described the importance of community and supporting one another. The imprint that was left deep within my heart from this beautiful conversation were her parting words: 'We are not home until everyone is home'. What could be more important for the future of our world than what is often described as 'walking each other home'.

In her work, Caroline Myss has created a unique set of archetypes. Archetypes have been around since Plato and Carl Jung was responsible for putting them on the map and world of psychology and modern consciousness. I use the following archetypes in my work with women. Many of the archetypes with shadow attributes we can find ourselves connected with include the Servant, the Victim, the Saboteur, and the Martyr. In transformation we can pivot to the Goddess, Warrior, Queen, and Visionary. Most women who have grown up in a religious background or educational system know of only two of the feminine archetypes: Mother Mary—the Virgin—archetype, and Mary Magdalene—the Prostitute—archetype. We can feel totally limited to looking up on these two archetypes in our reach for power in the world. Therefore, as women we step in and out of these two restricted archetypes and can box our sisters in likewise. The good news is there is a banquet of archetypes to choose from when stepping into our powers. And you get to choose. Here are the core archetypes I find helpful and supportive in my personal transformation and when supporting my clients to pivot.

Pivot from	To
Child Wounded	Child Magical
Child Orphan	Child Nature
Servant	Goddess
Victim	Warrior
Saboteur	Queen
Martyr	Visionary

It is safe now to let this old, dominating, limiting system go and with it any regret of wrongdoing. It is a time to embrace women's continued embracement of equality, and equality for everyone who may feel ill-treated, less than, or marginalised. We harbour the hope that the world is becoming a better place every day. We women are getting stronger at leaning in to each other, creating sisterhoods, and rising to dismantle the patriarchy. Feminine power is indeed breaking out in the rise of women—and of all genders—in the world.

May we release the wounds of our past together for all the women in the world who suffered abuse emotionally, physically, sexually, or spiritually at the hands of a patriarchal society. And for all the men who have been denied their human rights to feel and connect emotionally in the world. May we forgive the contribution that each of us may have made to the power of patriarchy in our lives. The *Ho'oponopono* is an ancient Hawaiian practice for forgiveness and reconciliation. It is a soothing process of reciting to make all things right with the earth, ancestors, others, and you. These special words allow forgiveness to flow apparently both ways.

The Ho'oponopono Prayer

I'm sorry.

Please forgive me.

Thank you.

I love you.

Honour Your Monthly Cycle

The path to power is in connection to your body, being in your body, and respecting your body. Our bodies carry our stories, memories, and emotions. We therefore need to nurture these valuable vehicles. Consider nourishing your body daily with movement, good nutrition, and positive affirmations. Remember it is eavesdropping on every word you speak and every thought you choose.

Women can increase their power by tuning in to the rhythm and changes of their menstrual cycles. We can learn to work with the cycles of the moon and our own inner seasons that are presented in the monthly cycle. Our daily lives and productivity can be supported by knowing the exact times to rest or create, engage or isolate, and the exact time to set that date for an important launch or event. Menstrual cycle awareness can honour the power within as opposed to viewing this creative cycle as an inconvenience; and I have heard it referred to as worse than that. The use of contraceptive implants will, of course, affect our ability to connect and optimise this power within, therefore disconnecting us from our inner GPS and natural cycle.

The Inner Seasons of the Monthly Cycle

Relax into your cycle and follow the flow. Each season has key tasks for you to optimise your superpowers.

> Inner Winter: *Seeds,* week 1, days 1–6—New moon/low tide; menstruation, a time to rest

> Inner Spring: *Shoots,* week 2, days 7–13—Waxing moon/incoming tide; preovulation, a time to inspire

> Inner Summer: *Flower,* week 3, days 14–21—Full moon/high tide; ovulation, a time to create

> Inner Autumn: *Leaves shed,* week 4, days 22–28—Waning moon/outgoing tide; post-ovulation, a time to refine

How reassuring that we do not have to be creating and producing every single day. We have an ebb and flow, the law of rhythm. More and more women all over the world are writing about this, embracing it, and positively transforming and optimising women's health, body wisdom, contributions, and achievements. It is a lot to ask from oneself to be in flower every day.

Women's power and wisdom depend on the connections with their bodies and owning all aspects of creativity and power to procreate. I am not just referring to the birthing of a child but birthing any creative form into the world—your baby! Trust that process; listen to your body. Birthing any idea or creation requires that sense of being and art of allowing with a sense of surrender, and trusting the law of gestation within a process rather than pushing against the flow of the natural tide. A labour of love is a gentle process, and just like delivering a baby, it can feel intense when close to birthing and the time to give one last big push at the end. When we birth and create, the exhilaration is so wonderful we immediately forget the pain threshold that we had to break through and know we can continue to create and achieve over and over again. We trust the process because the divine is deep within each and every one of us. It is activated in stillness and close encounters with oneself and we are reminded of it by the divine order of nature, especially our own radiant and divine nature, giving birth to the most powerful you.

Women of the world, know you are powerful beyond belief. Never settle for less than. Do not accept any condescension or degradation of women, whether in a serious or joking form. As Michelle Obama quite famously said, 'When they go low, we go high.' Pay attention to anything the world reflects to you, and let that be your inner work so that you continue to weed out anything that might contaminate and get in the way of your ability to bloom. Lift yourself up, raise other women up, and leave no women behind. Let's work harder than ever to raise girls and women up together all over the world. If we leave the women and children behind, we risk losing society's heartbeat.

Bloom because you are beautiful in so many, many ways. I see you, I hear you, and I love you. You are a radiant goddess. It is time for you to bloom, girl.

ACKNOWLEDGEMENTS

To everyone who has supported me throughout my healing journey.

Thank you for believing in me.

Printed and bound by CPI Group (UK) Ltd, Croydon, CR0 4YY